NO WAY TO RUN AN ECONOMY

NO WAY TO RUN AN ECONOMY

Why the System Failed and How to Put it Right

GRAHAM TURNER

PLUTO PRESS
www.plutobooks.com

First published 2009 by Pluto Press
345 Archway Road, London N6 5AA and
175 Fifth Avenue, New York, NY 10010

www.plutobooks.com

Distributed in the United States of America exclusively by
Palgrave Macmillan, a division of St. Martin's Press LLC,
175 Fifth Avenue, New York, NY 10010

British Library Cataloguing in Publication Data
A catalogue record for this book is available from the British Library

ISBN   978 0 7453 2977 2   Hardback
ISBN   978 0 7453 2976 5   Paperback

Library of Congress Cataloging in Publication Data applied for

This book is printed on paper suitable for recycling and made from
fully managed and sustained forest sources. Logging, pulping and
manufacturing processes are expected to conform to the environmental
standards of the country of origin. The paper may contain up to
70 per cent post-consumer waste.

10   9   8   7   6   5   4   3   2   1

Designed and produced for Pluto Press by
Chase Publishing Services Ltd, 33 Livonia Road, Sidmouth EX10 9JB, England
Typeset from disk by Stanford DTP Services, Northampton, England
Printed and bound in the European Union by
CPI Antony Rowe, Chippenham and Eastbourne

CONTENTS

LIST OF TABLES AND FIGURES

Table

Figures

GLOSSARY

Asset inflation – A continuous rise in either property prices or the stock market.

Average earnings – Monthly average wages or salaries, per person.

BAA bonds – Medium risk bonds, neither highly-protected nor poorly-secured.

Bank of England – Central bank of the United Kingdom.

Bank of Japan – Central bank of Japan.

Base metals – Industrial non-ferrous metals, including aluminium, copper, lead, nickel, tin and zinc.

Bretton Woods – The Bretton Woods system of monetary management established the rules for commercial and financial relations among the world's major industrial states in 1944.

Capacity utilisation – The percentage of capacity within industry being used for production.

Charge-off rate – The value of loans and leases removed from the books of banks and charged against loss reserves, net of recoveries.

Consols – A British government bond (gilt), dating from the eighteenth century.

Credit easing – The purchase of riskier assets by a central bank in an attempt to influence the price and, therefore, the implied yield on these assets.

Debt deflation – High levels of debt leading to falling asset prices and possibly negative inflation.

Debt trap – Attempts to pay off outstanding loans leading to a higher debt burden, as a result of the negative impact on prices.

Deflation – The opposite of inflation, a continuous fall in prices.

Delinquencies – Borrowers missing repayments on debt and falling into arrears.

EA 16 – Euro Area of 16 countries: Belgium, Germany, Ireland, Greece, Spain, France, Italy, Cyprus, Luxembourg, Malta, the Netherlands, Austria, Portugal, Slovenia, Slovakia and Finland.

European Central Bank – Central bank of the 16 countries in the Euro Area.

Fannie Mae – Formally called the Federal National Mortgage Association, Fannie Mae was founded in 1938, to facilitate mortgages to low income families. It was privatised in 1968.

Federal Open Market Committee (FOMC) – The FOMC of the Federal Reserve is responsible for US monetary policy.

Federal Reserve – Central bank of the US.

Foreclosure – Properties are foreclosed when borrowers default and banks repossess the asset.

Freddie Mac – The Federal Home Loan Mortgage Corporation is a government sponsored enterprise of the US federal government, created in 1970 to compete with Fannie Mae and expand the secondary market for mortgages in the US.

Free gold – Under the Gold Standard, US law specified that the Federal Reserve hold against notes a reserve of 40 per cent in gold and additional collateral of 60 per cent in either gold or eligible paper. Free gold was the amount over and above these requirements.

Gilt – UK government bond, issued to fund its borrowing.

Gold Standard – A commitment by participating countries to fix the price of domestic currencies in relation to gold.

Gross domestic product (GDP) – A broad indicator reflecting the size of an economy, usually in terms of output, but also in terms of spending and income.

GSE-backed securities – Government Sponsored Enterprise mortgage-backed securities. Mortgage-backed securities represent an investment in mortgage loans. An MBS investor owns an interest in a pool of mortgages, which serves as the underlying assets and source of cash flow for the security.

Inflation – A continuous rise in prices.

Keynes – Policies of Keynes emphasise the role of monetary policy, including lower short-term interest rates, bond buying and debt management operations in an attempt to control long-term borrowing costs. They also include the implementation of capital and lending controls to facilitate the control of interest rates.

Keynesian – Keynesian policies refer to the use of fiscal policy ahead of monetary weapons to control the economy.

Large-scale open market purchases – see *Open market purchases*.

Libor – The London Interbank Offered Rate is a daily reference rate based on the interest rate at which banks borrow unsecured funds from other banks in the London wholesale money market or interbank market.

Liquidity trap – A liquidity trap occurs when long-term government bond yields can no longer fall by natural means and have reached a point of resistance, due to investors' risk aversion.

Monetary base – A narrow measure of money supply including notes and coins in circulation plus bank reserves.

Moral hazard – The prospect that a party insulated from risk may behave differently from the way it would behave if it were fully exposed to the risk.

New York Fed – Federal Reserve Bank of New York.

Open market purchases – A central bank buys assets as part of its monetary policy, in an attempt to influence the price and the implied yield on the assets. Large-scale open market purchases were routinely executed in the operation of monetary policy in the 1920s and 1930s.

Overinvestment – Where capital or investment spending has reached a high and unsustainable proportion of the economy.

Public-Private Investment Program – A US administration initiative to remove the bad debts from the books of banks by offering generous subsidies to private sector asset managers.

Quantitative easing – A monetary policy weapon where a central bank buys assets – government bonds – to influence the yield and borrowing costs more generally.

Savings and Loan – Specialised banks created to fund and promote homeownership in the US after the Second World War.

Structured investment vehicles – A pool of investment assets, which attempts to profit from spreads between short-term debt and long-term structured finance products, such as asset-backed securities.

Treasuries or **Treasury** – US government bond or debt, issued to fund its borrowing.

U6 – U6 unemployment includes all individuals over 16, available for work and who have actively looked for work in the past four weeks, plus marginally attached and involuntary part-time workers. Marginally attached to the labour force includes individuals who wanted and were available for work and had looked for a job sometime in the past twelve months. These individuals were not counted as unemployed as they had not looked for work in the previous four weeks. Involuntary part-time workers includes individuals working less than 35 hours per week for economic reasons, that is, poor business conditions or an inability to find full-time work.

Zero bound – Refers to the practical impossibility of negative interest rates.

GFC ECONOMICS

GFC Economics is an independent economic consultancy based in London, founded in 1999.

For more information, please email
Pat Sharp at pat.sharp@gfceconomics.com or
Graham Turner at graham.turner@gfceconomics.com or
visit the website at www.gfceconomics.com.

ACKNOWLEDGEMENTS

All charts are provided courtesy of Thomson Reuters Datastream.

Graham Turner would like to thank Pat Sharp for her invaluable assistance with production of charts and editing. Thanks also to Joseph Choonara and Geoff Tily for reading and commenting on some of this material. Thanks once again to Vanessa Rossi at Chatham House for her econometric skills. Thanks to Laura Staples for her research assistance. Finally, thanks to my partner Jackie. Hours of discussion have helped shape a coherent view of the world.

Any errors or omissions are entirely the responsibility of the author.

Solutions to a Liquidity Trap: Japan's Bear Market and What it Means for the West

Published by GFC Economics, June 2003

Solutions to a Liquidity Trap is an in-depth analysis of Japan's long bear market and examines in detail the policy mistakes made by the Japanese authorities as they battled against more than a decade of deflation. It contains a strong historical narrative of all the financial crises that erupted from 1990 onwards, in chronological order, including a detailed record of all the key bankruptcies that wreaked so much havoc.

To order a copy of *Solutions to a Liquidity Trap*, please send a cheque for £20 (includes postage and packaging) to GFC Economics, Coburn House, 3 Coburn Road, Bow, London E3 2DA.

The Credit Crunch: Housing Bubbles, Globalisation and the Worldwide Economic Crisis

Published by Pluto Press, June 2008, £14.99

The Credit Crunch examines the pitfalls within globalisation leading to the financial crisis that rocked the world economy in the autumn of 2008. When it was published, *The Credit Crunch* warned that central banks and governments were underestimating the potential difficulties that lay ahead. It examined the parallels with Japan and argued for a more urgent policy response, to 'prevent debt deflation taking root'.

INTRODUCTION

'Change We Need' became the popularised slogan during President Obama's emotional election campaign. Change was certainly needed. But nothing changed in the critical early months following the handover. President Obama's economic policies were indistinguishable from those of the Bush era. In critical respects, they were worse. The US – and by extension the rest of the world – remained in deep trouble, because policymakers had digested few of the important lessons of history. And they were unwilling to effect the radical policies needed.

Share prices did rally from the lows reached in March 2009 as financial markets sensed a reprieve. It seemed that determined attempts to reflate, driven by huge interest rate cuts, massive bailouts for banks, increased public spending and tax cuts, were percolating through.

It may well prove to be a false dawn. All the evidence suggested that the US economy was enjoying a limited, short-lived boost from tax rebates. Indeed, by the end of June 2009, the impact of Obama's fiscal largesse was already beginning to fade.[1] Debt deflation, propelled by falling house prices, remained entrenched.

If the world economy relapses in 2010, the policy options will be few *under the current economic system*. There will be few conventional policy weapons left to bring the patient back to life. Interest rates down to virtually zero and budget deficits soaring to post-war highs across the industrialised world have left scant room for manoeuvre.

The omens are hardly encouraging. Foreclosure filings hit record highs in the US in the three months to May 2009.[2] Burdened by a huge inventory of repossessed homes, banks have resorted to mass sales through auction houses, fuelling price destruction on an unprecedented scale. But in many cases, empty properties are being returned to banks, unsold, left empty and abandoned. In

1

California, one of the worst affected states, one in eight homes sent to auction was left unsold in May 2009, despite most properties being offered at discounts of more than 50 per cent.[3]

Attempts by banks to eliminate their toxic assets by selling foreclosed homes are creating more bad debts. Falling house prices are pushing more homeowners into negative equity, triggering more defaults and more repossessions. It's a vicious cycle, worse than Japan's debt trap in the 1990s and with no end in sight.

Unemployment has continued its relentless climb under Obama. Another 467,000 jobs disappeared in June alone, worse than any month in the previous three recessions.[4] The economy remains in recession as fear stalks those shopping malls still open. The era of easy credit is over and the profligacy of the boom years is not coming back (see Figure 0.1).

——— $ Billion, Monthly Change, Averaged Over Three Months

Figure 0.1   US Consumer Credit

Source: Federal Reserve

The Federal Reserve mistimed its rate cuts in response to the housing crisis. It could and should have acted much sooner. A pre-emptive policy might have eliminated some of the distress seen today. The Bank of England and the European Central Bank were also too slow. All three central banks were wrong to allow credit growth to spiral out of control in the first place. But through their inaction, they are also guilty of facilitating the worst economic contraction in the post-war era.[5]

— % Change year-on-year

Figure 0.2   US Real GDP

Source: Department of Commerce

When the consequences of their malign neglect became apparent in February 2007, the central banks – and governments – dithered. They seemed unable to comprehend that their policies would precipitate serial banking crises, paralysing the financial

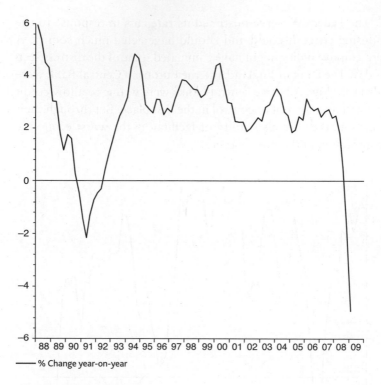

Figure 0.3   UK Real GDP

Source: Office for National Statistics

system. They utterly underestimated the scale of the looming economic collapse.

Following the demise of the US investment bank Bear Stearns in March 2008, interest rates should have been cut aggressively. Quantitative easing – driving long-term interest rates lower – was critical too. However, it was clear that if central banks did not use this most important of monetary weapons early in the crisis, it was unlikely to work either. By July 2009, the US had reached that point. A limited stab at quantitative easing had failed to reverse the economic decline.

The Bank of England was pushing harder than any other central bank, but the UK is not an economic island. Its fortunes remain indelibly tied to the US through its extreme dependency

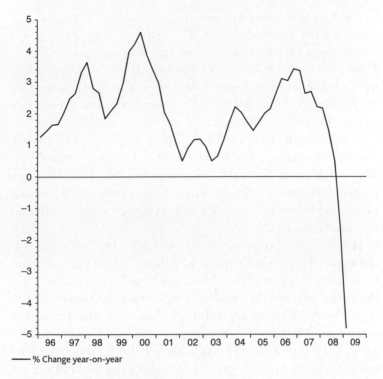

Figure 0.4 Euroland Real GDP

Source: Eurostat

on financial markets to drive the economy. If the Federal Reserve fails, the UK will flounder too.

The whole world still relies on the US consumer, as events of the past year have shown. Chinese attempts to compensate and drag the rest of the world out of recession depend on more of the same policies that got the West into trouble – ramping up bank lending. By the spring of 2009, even the Chinese leaders were beginning to doubt the wisdom of an Anglo Saxon strategy.[6]

Banking on Obama

By the spring of 2009, the Obama administration had five planks to its strategy of reflation. None of them was working.

The first was monetary policy. Zero interest rates had not stabilised the housing market. The collapse in property prices became so endemic, that interest rate cuts stopped working. Quantitative easing also came too late. It was not introduced until a year after the collapse of Bear Stearns and six months after the demise of Lehman Brothers. Even then, there was a reluctance to push the policy to its limits.

In between the two, the Federal Reserve pioneered a middle way, 'credit easing'. The impact of that has been limited too. Worse still, going down this route deflected the Federal Reserve from implementing more aggressive quantitative easing, the one policy that helped to reverse the slide in economic activity during the summer of 1932.

The second plank involved yet more liquidity injections into the financial system, a projected $1 trillion, via the Public-Private Investment Program (PPIP). However, liquidity injections target the symptoms, not the cause of a debt crisis. Previous liquidity injections by Western central banks had been unsuccessful in turning the tide because borrowing costs had not been cut quickly enough. This latest attempt was likely to fall short too. Indeed, by late June, leading US newspapers were declaring the PPIP as dead and unworkable. The banks were unable to participate because it would force them to book large losses as they sold their devalued assets. And they did not have the capacity on their balance sheets to absorb yet more losses.[7]

The third involved a belated attempt by US lenders to modify mortgages on a piecemeal basis. Previous programmes had failed miserably and the latest effort was likely to prove inadequate. Millions of homeowners were too deep in negative equity for loan modifications to work. Rising unemployment also meant large numbers of debtors had no income to make modifications possible. And where they were possible, many soon ran into trouble again, defaulting.[8]

The fourth, involved yet more fiscal expansion, piling 'debt upon debt', resorting to so-called Keynesian policies. But the US authorities failed to understand the prescription set out by John Maynard Keynes in the 1930s. Large budget deficits at the expense of lower borrowing costs are counterproductive. They are likely to ensure the West remains mired in a debt trap beyond 2009. Lastly came the ultimate charade, the stress tests. Banks were asked to prove they had sufficient capital to survive a worst case economic scenario. Along with the accountancy gimmickry waved through by the Federal regulators under Obama's watch, it was a blatant attempt to manipulate stock market sentiment.[9] When all other options have failed, hoodwinking becomes an important policy weapon in its own right.

Looking to 2010

Banks will modify some mortgages to appease critics, but left in the private realm their primary duty will remain to shareholders. They will continue to repossess in large numbers, overwhelming the auction houses. By April 2009, the average US house price across ten major cities had dropped 33.6 per cent from its peak. A fall of 60 per cent from peak to trough no longer seems outlandish. A drop of 70 per cent would take prices down to levels not seen since 1987.[10] But this destruction of paper 'wealth' will further depress the economy.[11]

The cycle will not be broken by the policies adopted by President Obama in his early months. He will have to change course. His administration cannot be blamed for the mistakes of the Bush era. The huge rise in unemployment immediately following the collapse of Lehman Brothers is not the fault of the current president. But Obama can be cited for carrying on with the same failed policies of his predecessor, which have continued to drive the jobless total higher.

The Obama administration's avowed intention is to keep the banks in the private sector. It remains wedded to a free market ideology.[12] Obama is a centrist. He has surrounded himself with pro-market economists, such as Paul Volcker, the former Federal Reserve chair. Volcker was embraced enthusiastically during the Obama election campaign.[13] Obama appealed to the masses to build his movement for change, but no other individual did more to break the power of ordinary working class Americans during the early 1980s.

The determination to keep the banks in the private sector is failing the US. Left to their own devices, banks will continue to drive endemic property deflation and economic decline. The US will pay a heavy price for Obama's ideological dogmatism. But the causes of this crisis cannot be solved merely by nationalising banks. This book's predecessor, *The Credit Crunch*, identified both globalisation and the concerted attempt to drive wage costs lower as key culprits behind the build-up in debt across many Western economies.[14] The surge in borrowing was possible because cheap imports kept inflation low. The emergence of a dominant class of multinationals, outsourcing and driving labour costs down reinforced the cycle.

Low inflation made housing bubbles possible. But the compression of wages ensured they were a necessary driver of economic growth too. To see the record debt burden as simply a failure of regulation or a lax monetary policy ignores the underlying causes of the economic crisis.

Viewed through this prism, it is quite clear the policy mistakes that turned a series of banking failures into a deep recession were not simply a failure of individuals. It is right to criticise Ben Bernanke, the Federal Reserve chair, and other policymakers for their inability to react in time. They clearly erred.

But history is repeating itself. Many of the mistakes made from 2007 onwards were identical to the policy errors committed in the early 1930s, which turned a stock market crash into a depression. In some cases, the policy mistakes today have been worse. Under Ben Bernanke, the Federal Reserve has failed to learn from the Great Depression. A policy of reflation that began under President Hoover and continued under President Roosevelt secured a recovery, even if it ultimately stalled in 1937. The policies of 2009 remain inadequate to reverse the slump.

If we cannot learn from history, it is time to consider deeper causes for the crisis. Policy mistakes have not been governed by individuals. Central bankers and politicians failed to anticipate the looming crisis, because they were embedded within an economic philosophy that sees the domination of large corporations as the only driver for economic growth. If they understood the role of big business in driving the debt bubble, they might have responded quickly to the collapse of house prices.

They believed that companies were doing well, so the economy was fundamentally sound. They could see no alternative. And so they failed to see the flaws of a system they helped to create and tried to control – until it spun out of their grasp.

They now seek to regroup using conventional policy weapons, and for a short while their actions have appeared successful. But each and every crisis since early 2007 has reduced the scope for governments and central banks to respond when the next bout of turbulence hits financial markets. When the world economy starts to slip again, there will be nowhere to go within the current ideology. Real change will then have to be foisted upon our elected representatives.

State control is not enough and certainly not a panacea. Big business and finance are well equipped to use the state to reinforce their dominance. State intervention with today's democratic deficit will maintain the status quo. Democratic accountability implies holding more than politicians to account. It has to begin in the workplace and our public institutions. It means rejecting the shareholder model that allows companies to roam the globe cutting labour costs in the name of free trade, compressing wages and driving debt up. It means holding banks to account for their predatory actions in throwing millions out of their homes, plunging the US – and thus the rest of the world – deeper into crisis.

And it means confronting governments and big business for their neglect of the biggest threat to the planet – climate change. The credit crunch has been exacerbated by the failures of policymakers wedded to an out-of-date economic ideology. We should be under no illusion that these governments have the answers, or willingness, to meet the challenge of reducing carbon emissions.

This book is ultimately a warning. It shows that our policymakers got it wrong, not because they were stupid. They drove the world economy into its deepest post-war recession because the economic system prevented them from seeing its flaws. Their blind pursuit of the profit model drove the biggest housing collapse in the history of capitalism. It distorted their vision of the real world, the struggles facing ordinary workers and the impact of their policies on the real economy. It may irretrievably damage the planet too.

Chapter 1 begins with the collapse of Bear Stearns. It charts the policy actions of central banks and governments during the spring and summer of 2008 that led directly to the collapse of Lehman Brothers. The demise of a second investment bank within six months was not inevitable. But it was catastrophic.

Even then, there was time to row back. But as we show in Chapter 2, the response of the Federal Reserve in 2008 was very different from that in 1932, when the US economy began its long, slow road to rehabilitation. It was wrong and less effective. The policies implemented in the first six months of 2009 remain a huge barrier to economic recovery.

In Chapter 3, we argue that central banks and governments have failed to understand the prescription put forward by Keynes in the 1930s. Using fiscal policy to cut taxes and ramp up government spending at the first sign of trouble is not the policy advocated by Keynes. However, politicians were so desperate to prop up their discredited model that they distorted Keynes to justify their policy response. Their misunderstanding of history will thus compound the crisis.

In Chapter 4, we warn that the destructive forces unleashed by globalisation have not gone away despite the credit crunch. Indeed, they are intensifying and will undermine the ability of governments and central banks to deliver meaningful economic recovery.

In Chapter 5, we take a look at a Marxist critique of the crisis. The dynamics of the economic contraction that began in 2008, with many companies saddled with huge excess capacity, underlines a key problem with capitalism – the incessant drive for market share and overaccumulation.

In Chapter 6, we offer some comparisons between the Marx critique and the Keynes prescription. Ultimately, the failure of policymakers to learn even some of the most basic lessons of the early 1930s is not the fault of individuals. Instead, it reflects deep-seated problems with the economic system.

In chapter 7, we argue that the Obama administration may find it impossible to break out of the current debt trap without nationalising banks. Indeed, putting banks into the public realm would act as a 'circuit breaker', and would be a much more effective policy weapon against persistent property deflation and soaring repossessions. It has become a necessary policy weapon. But the Obama administration is ideologically opposed to such a step, and that will impoverish the US and the rest of the world economy.

Finally in Chapter 8, there are some suggestions for real change. An urgent debate has erupted over how to deliver a radical shift in the economy towards one less prone to boom and bust. Some of the resolutions put forward elsewhere will inevitably not go far enough. They have been proffered by those who failed to anticipate much of the recent carnage, and merely wish to preserve the status quo.

Readers will have their own ideas and suggestions, many of which will deserve scrutiny. Ultimately, the key is democratic accountability, to make change happen, to avoid a repeat of the mistakes of the past three decades. Today's younger generation will be paying for our collective mistakes for years. We owe it to them to effect real change, to bring an end to boom and bust. Before that can happen, we have to fix the current crisis. And that objective remains far from secured.

1

FROM BEAR STEARNS TO RECESSION

'Time is running out for the Federal Reserve' was the blunt assessment in early April 2008 as *The Credit Crunch* went to print.[1] Borrowing costs, in particular mortgage rates, had to be targeted and driven lower, through a mixture of deep rate cuts and quantitative easing. Otherwise, more banks would fail and depression could follow recession. Delay would prove costly.

Governments and central banks had to act quickly to prevent debt deflation from taking root. But after a bankrupt Bear Stearns had been sold to JP Morgan in March 2008, policymakers and politicians sat back. They did little to arrest the downward spiral in house prices and the inevitable slide into deep recession. Bear Stearns was a one-off, they thought. They switched tack, fretting about inflation when the real threat was the Japanese curse of falling prices and multiple banking failures.

That was hard to square with the evidence. By the time the US had lost the first of its five major investment banks, 238 mortgage companies had already gone out of business.[2] More banks were certain to fail if the Federal Reserve did not try to stabilise the property market. Bad debts would continue to accumulate causing shareholders to flee banks and sparking depositor runs.

Federal Reserve Chair Ben Bernanke has since claimed that the Federal Reserve 'responded aggressively to the crisis since its emergence in the summer of 2007'. The policy response was 'exceptionally rapid and proactive' in historical comparison, he has argued.[3]

The Fed had allowed money supply to contract during 1930 and 1931, amplifying the initial fallout of the stock market crash a year earlier and turning a recession into depression.[4] The contrast with the supposedly more proactive policy adopted from the summer of 2007 onwards showed the Fed had learnt the lessons that would prevent another economic slump.

In reality, Ben Bernanke's Fed made precisely the same mistakes that fuelled the Great Depression. Huge numbers of banks defaulted a year after the stock market crash in 1929, notably in Missouri, Indiana, Illinois, Iowa, Arkansas and North Carolina. In November 1930, 256 banks failed and a month later another 352 banks collapsed, including the Bank of United States.[5] Very little was done to prevent their demise.

The decline in money supply was driven by the loss of these banks. As they failed, credit suddenly became scarce and the decline in asset prices accelerated. More banks collapsed and the economy spiralled deeper into recession.

In this critical respect, the latter months of 2006 and early 2007 were no different from 1930 or 1931. The implosion of so many mortgage originators from 2006 onwards similarly accelerated the decline in the availability of credit. The failure of the Federal Reserve to act when these lenders collapsed turned what might have been a soft landing into a crash.

Indeed, it is perhaps notable that Ben Bernanke claims the summer of 2007 marks the starting point of the crisis. For many financial market participants the crisis began in February 2007 following profit warnings in the US from HSBC and New Century Financial.[6] For huge numbers of US homeowners struggling to meet debt repayments, the problems started two years before that. Indeed, sub-prime borrowers were in trouble even before interest rates started to rise during 2004.[7]

Federal Reserve data should have alerted the US authorities to the risks of a hard landing. At the peak of the boom in Q3 2005, $631.5 billion of new mortgage-backed bonds were issued to fund the lending frenzy.[8] Throughout 2006, the pace of issuance dropped progressively. By the third quarter of 2006, it had already fallen by nearly a fifth. As mortgage originators started to fold, issuance fell sharply in the final quarter, by just over a third from a year earlier. And it carried on sliding during the first half of 2007.[9]

By the third quarter of 2007, the disappearance of so many lenders, combined with a reluctance of investors to buy mortgage bonds, had caused issuance to collapse to *minus* $232.4 billion (see Figure 1.1). Mortgage funding from these bonds – a critical driver of the housing boom – had not just slowed. It was contracting.

This was a stunning reversal and without precedent in modern times. It represented a shrinkage and collapse of money supply similar to that seen in the first year of the Great Depression. History was repeating itself.[10]

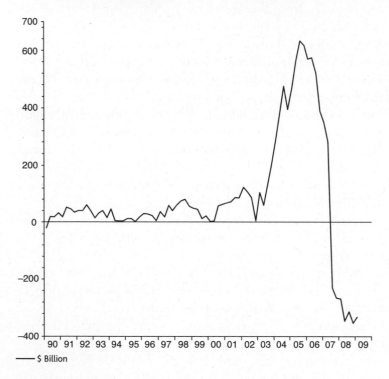

Figure 1.1   US Asset Backed Securities, Residential Mortgages

Source: Federal Reserve

The Inflation 'Crisis'

The Federal Reserve governors of 1930 and 1931 were also unwilling to support the banks. They tended to view bank failures as 'regrettable consequences of bad management and bad banking practices'.[11] They were also 'beholden' to the Gold Standard because it was considered to be the ultimate bulwark against inflation.

The Fed of 2007 and 2008 overestimated the inflation risks too, with tragic consequences for millions who would lose their jobs and homes. The Fed was not alone. The Bank of England and the European Central Bank also failed to comprehend the true threat facing the world economy.

Superficially, it did appear as if the policymakers had a point. By March 2008, inflation had risen to 4.0 per cent in the US, 2.4 per cent in the UK and 3.5 per cent in Euroland. Oil and food prices were soaring. Over the summer, inflation would climb to a high of 5.6 per cent in the US. It would more than double in the UK, rising to 5.2 per cent by September. And in Euroland, it would accelerate to more than twice the European Central Bank's target, jumping to 4.1 per cent by July.[12]

The debate over runaway commodity prices was polarised. Some saw this as a manifestation of loose monetary policies in the West and particularly emerging market economies.[13] Central banks in the West would have to hike interest rates further, it was claimed, to compensate for the unwillingness of policymakers to tame a surge in inflation across emerging market economies. Across Eastern Europe, Asia, Latin America, the Middle East and Africa, inflation was accelerating, climbing well into double digits in many countries.

Some economists highlighted the specific supply problems that had contributed to big cost increases. Peak Oil, the growth of biofuels and climate change were held responsible for the surge in energy and food costs. However, metals and other non-food and energy commodity prices were also rising sharply in response to strong emerging market demand.

But the longer-term or secular threat to inflation was far from clear-cut. Much of the rapid growth in emerging market demand reflected domestic credit bubbles that in many cases were more extreme than in the West. When they burst, demand for commodities would collapse taking prices down swiftly.

And so it proved. Having more than doubled in three years, base metal prices finally peaked on 5 March 2008. Oil prices reached their zenith on 11 July.[14] As the world economy lurched towards recession, the reversal was swift and brutal. By the end of 2008, base metals had tumbled 60 per cent and oil had fallen 75 per cent. Overall, commodity prices had slumped by 61 per cent from their 2008 high (see Figure 1.2).[15] Even with food and energy excluded, they had still dropped 39 per cent. Furthermore, non-energy commodity prices had peaked in March *before* Bear Stearns failed.[16]

—— Goldman Sachs Commodity Price Index, Total

Figure 1.2   Commodity Prices

Source: Thomson Reuters Datastream

Inflation proved not to be the danger portrayed by many. It did rise in the first half of 2008. But this never marked a shift to the inflationary spiral that bedevilled the 1970s or 1980s.

Central banks – and many politicians for that matter – massively overstated the inflation threat. Employers were unwilling to raise wage rates in line with the acceleration in consumer prices. Many companies still had the upper hand, and the choice was simple: higher wages would mean more jobs would be lost to overseas. Today's globalised economy had irrevocably altered the inflation dynamics. As a result, incomes fell sharply in real terms. There were no 'second-round effects' typical of the 1970s and 1980s.[17] High levels of borrowing also limited the ability of workers to absorb cost shocks, such as surging oil prices and utility bills. Debt was the new slavery.

Through the summer of 2008, central bankers inveighed against the threat of higher wages, arguing that their priority was to bring inflation back under control. Only that would underpin financial stability, they claimed. After being lambasted for allowing credit growth to spin out of control during the boom, central banks belatedly relished the opportunity to act tough, resisting pleas to do more to arrest the housing slumps. They were following their mandate, and in the long run, the public would thank them for not deviating from their goal. Soon after the Bear Stearns collapse, interest rate hikes were back on the agenda.

But as the months rolled by, wage settlements and pay rates barely shifted.[18] Policymakers had switched their focus to fight a phoney war, with catastrophic consequences for the housing market, financial stability and the real economy.

The dogmatism of central banks was aided and abetted by a political class that saw fighting inflation as the key to the economic boom. They could not – or preferred not to – see that it was unrestrained credit growth, housing bubbles and out of control banks that had driven the long upswing. They were wedded to a broken and out-of-date ideology. Cost cutting, deregulation and the growth of free trade had been the cornerstones of economic policy throughout the West. And yet, these very policies had led ineluctably to rapid credit growth, which in turn, nullified the threat of inflation becoming embedded.[19]

Figure 1.3   US Average Hourly Earnings

Source: Bureau of Labor Statistics

The risks were clearly asymmetric. Oil prices might have been soaring, but eventually they would stop rising. Even if the world was running short of supplies, oil prices would eventually reach an equilibrium. Once they had levelled out, the lack of response from wages implied inflation would then fall quickly.

By overreacting to the rise in commodity prices, central banks accelerated the collapse into deep recession. Through their misjudgement or ideological dogmatism, they amplified the slide into deflation. The slump in commodity prices, when it arrived, would prove precipitous because demand was crushed by an inappropriate monetary policy. Even if the Peak Oil theory was right, the fall in demand would be so great that tight supplies at some point would prove irrelevant. And that moment would arrive even sooner than many expected.[20]

Many warnings were ignored. Core inflation, which excludes food and energy, moved higher in the US and UK, but the rise was limited. It peaked in 2008 at 2.5 per cent in the US and just 2.2 per cent in the UK. In the early 1980s, core inflation and RPIX hit highs of 13.6 per cent and 20.8 per cent respectively. In the early 1990s, it peaked at 5.6 per cent and 9.5 per cent respectively.[21]

—— % Change year-on-year

Figure 1.4   US Consumer Prices Ex-Food/Energy

Source: Bureau of Labor Statistics

There was even less excuse for the policy blunders committed by the European Central Bank. Core inflation peaked at just 2.0 per cent in March 2008. The rise in inflation above the 2.0 per cent target was exclusively due to oil and food prices.[22]

Furthermore, there were some elements of core inflation that were palpably affected by higher oil prices. They would stop rising as soon as oil prices levelled out. Airfares were a case in point. This had significant impact on core inflation, but airfares soon went into reverse as oil prices tumbled.[23]

There was considerable anecdotal evidence to suggest higher commodity prices were not inflationary too. Discount retailers were experiencing a boom. In the UK, cost-cutting supermarkets Aldi and Lidl were notable beneficiaries of an underlying price squeeze. Suffering deep wage cuts, many workers were trading down, substituting and switching to cheaper alternatives. High-value stores, such as Marks & Spencer, suffered a disproportionate

—— % Change year-on-year

Figure 1.5   UK Retail Sales Deflator

Source: Office for National Statistics

decline in sales. Other retailers reported a sudden rise in price-conscious shoppers, buying cheaper and, of course, less healthy brands.[24] And the trend accelerated in the early months of 2008. Business was booming at 'run-down stores' and street markets were enjoying a resurgence. With unemployment rising, hard-pressed consumers were turning their backs on mainstream stores.[25]

The severe pressure on retailers was self-evident from the official data. The Office for National Statistics in the UK publishes an alternative measure of inflation – the *retail sales deflator*. The retail sales deflator is a measure of price changes based on a changing basket of goods.[26] By contrast, the Consumer Price Index (CPI) assumes shopping habits remain static every year. As a result, the

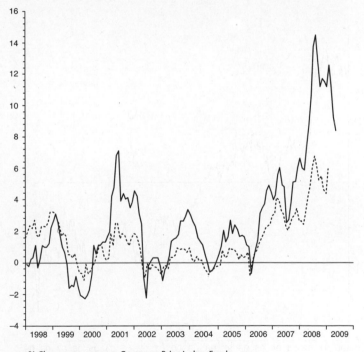

Figure 1.6   UK Food Inflation

——— % Change year-on-year, Consumer Price Index, Food
– – % Change year-on-year, Retail Sales Deflator, Food Stores

Source: Office for National Statistics

deflators are more subtle. They had, for example, provided an early indication that inflation risks were beginning to subside in the West during the mid-1990s.[27]

As headline inflation accelerated in the UK from the spring onwards, the retail sales deflator flashed a warning. It remained stubbornly in negative territory until May 2008, and then rose to a high of just 2.1 per cent y/y three months later, before turning down again (see Figure 1.5). It was difficult to see how this could be construed as an inflation threat. In the early 1980s, the deflator had peaked at 16.5 per cent y/y. In the early 1990s it reached a high of 6.5 per cent y/y.[28]

Hard-pressed, cash-strapped shoppers weighed down by record debt levels and squeezed by falling real wages, were unable to

—— % Change year-on-year

Figure 1.7   UK Retail Sales Deflator, Non-Food Stores

Source: Office for National Statistics

afford the price increases reflected in the official CPI. Decomposing the retail sales deflator provided an insight into the impact of the credit squeeze on retailers and consumers. The CPI suggested that food prices were rising at an annual rate of 14.5 per cent by August 2008. By contrast, the retail sales deflator for food showed that once this switching to cheaper alternatives had been taken into account, the annual increase was much lower – just 6.7 per cent (see Figure 1.6). The same was true for non-food stores, where consumer resistance caused prices to fall by an average of 3.1 per cent y/y between January and August 2008 (see Figure 1.7). That compared with a drop of 1.4 per cent y/y on the comparable CPI measure.[29]

Bank of England Misjudges

None of this registered with the Bank of England. Its August 2008 inflation bulletin was littered with warnings. In the 52-page report released just weeks before the financial system went into meltdown, import inflation was cited 22 times, food prices 32 times, oil 32 times, while energy prices were referenced on 40 separate occasions.[30] The retail sales deflator was not mentioned once. The implicit squeeze on shoppers in response to falling real wages was discussed only briefly. Instead, the possibility that an increase in inflation expectations would feed through to higher wages was the predominant risk.[31]

Indeed, the Bank argued that real wages had to shrink otherwise there would be a more pronounced rise in unemployment. Falling real wages were the price workers had to pay to hold on to their jobs.[32] That unemployment would soar anyway because interest rates had been left too high for too long, was beyond the Bank's comprehension.

Along with so many others, Bank of England officials were oblivious to the realities of life for hard-pressed workers, and missed the true impact of globalisation on inflation. The one exception was Professor David Blanchflower, an expert in the labour market. He had been consistently warning of a sharp rise in unemployment, urging fellow members of the Monetary Policy

Committee to cut interest rates.[33] For much of 2008, his pleas went unanswered. For nine consecutive meetings between January and September, Mr Blanchflower dissented, urging rate cuts or voting for bigger reductions.[34]

By contrast, one Monetary Policy Committee member voted twice for rate hikes over the summer of 2008. Timothy Besley invoked the US detective programme *Starsky and Hutch* and the film *Saturday Night Fever*, as he hyped the perils of a return to the 1970s. Writing in the down-market *Sun* newspaper on 19 August 2008 – days before the credit crunch erupted for the fourth time – the London School of Economics professor claimed the pain from keeping interest rates high would be worthwhile. It would provide 'the best basis for the economy to grow, create jobs and allow living standards to rise' and he warned workers not to 'chase inflationary wage increases'.[35]

Andrew Sentance had been head of economic policy at the Confederation of British Industry before joining the Bank of England's Monetary Policy Committee. It was not difficult to imagine where his sympathies lay. He had been reluctant to cut rates earlier in the year, siding with Timothy Besley following the collapse of Bear Stearns, arguing for rates to be left on hold, when the rest of the Monetary Policy Committee could see the need for action.[36] Even after the collapse of Lehman Brothers, he was urging fellow Monetary Policy Committee members to 'stick to basics' and focus on the inflation target, while fretting over a 'wage-price spiral'.[37]

Fed Hawks

The Federal Reserve had its share of inflation 'hawks' too. Leading the cast was Richard Fisher, president of the Federal Reserve Bank of Dallas. Even as the housing market spiralled downwards, he voted against a rate cut in January, March and April 2008. As the Federal Reserve then left interest rates on hold, he voted for a rate hike in June and August. After the collapse of Lehman Brothers, he fell into line and voted for rate cuts, although the belated shift to lower borrowing costs proved insufficient to arrest the slide in stock markets.[38] Mr Fisher wanted to fix the credit system first, preferring alternative 'measures targeted at relieving liquidity strains'. That would 'improve economic prospects more quickly', he ventured.[39] It was the classic mistake made not only by dissenters, but by the majority of policymakers. Mr Fisher and others failed to see that liquidity strains were a second order problem derived from high borrowing costs.

Another hawk was the president of the Philadelphia Federal Reserve, Charles Plosser. He voted against rate cuts in March and April.[40] Explaining his dissent, Mr Plosser argued that 'Monetary policy cannot solve all the problems the economy and financial system now face.' That may well have been right, but not for the reasons Plosser imagined. He believed that the solution to the housing crisis lay with the 'market'. 'The markets will have to solve these problems', he claimed.[41]

A third dissenter was William Poole, head of the Federal Reserve Bank of Saint Louis. Mr Poole voted against the first of the two rate cuts in January 2008.[42] Like Mr Plosser, he believed that it was up to the market to resolve the mortgage crisis. More careful analysis of the underlying mortgages was needed by lenders. 'We can be confident that in time the market will straighten out the problems', he suggested.[43] Events would prove otherwise.

These dissents did not change the course of monetary policy and alone were not responsible for the subsequent collapse in financial markets. The failure to bring interest rates down quickly was the fault of all policymakers. But pushing for higher borrowing costs when the housing markets were in freefall did little to reassure an increasingly stressed and agitated financial system.

Driving Borrowing Costs Up

The threat of higher interest rates in both the US and UK over the summer of 2008 never materialised. Monetary policy remained on hold in both countries. But the damage was done. By talking tough, central banks still drove interest rate *expectations* up.[44]

That in turn had a profound impact on many private sector borrowing rates. Expectations play a pivotal role in determining borrowing costs. With rate expectations climbing, house prices in the US, UK and across much of Euroland were sure to continue spiralling down, taking more banks under. It was only a question of when financial markets would collapse under the weight of bad debts.

In Euroland, official interest rates actually went up in early July 2008, by 0.25 per cent to 4.25 per cent. The head of the European Central Bank, Jean-Claude Trichet, warned that further hikes would be necessary to drive inflation back down within target and claimed the backing of Europe's citizens.[45] One policy official, the head of Austria's central bank, the Oesterreichische Nationalbank, was looking forward to an economic recovery in the final months of 2008, suggesting there was room for yet more rate hikes.[46] The European Commission had few doubts over the wisdom of the European Central Bank's action. 'Inflation is really a threat and can really put in danger not only the European but the global economy', warned the Commission's president, Manuel Barroso.[47]

Subsequent data confirmed that Euroland had been in recession for more than three months before the final, misguided rate hike. The second quarter GDP report would show that the Euroland economy was already contracting.[48] European Central Bank governors would not have been in possession of these numbers when they decided to hike. But there was a swathe of indicators pointing to a collapse in consumer and business confidence. Retail spending was contracting, and even the previous GDP reports suggested that there had been a significant slowing of consumer spending since the summer of 2007 in response to the first freeze in money markets (see Figure 1.8).[49]

The next and far more damaging phase of the credit crunch was about to erupt. Stock markets had started to slide from May 2008 onwards. Over the summer the selling gathered momentum.[50] The failure of central banks to arrest the slump in house prices led investors to fear banks would run short of capital. The cycle was becoming eerily reminiscent of Japan's long slide into a debt trap

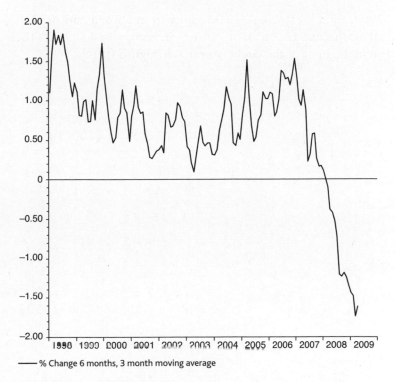

———— % Change 6 months, 3 month moving average

Figure 1.8   Euroland Retail Sales

Source: Eurostat

in the 1990s. Bank share prices were the canary in the coalmine. When investors lost faith in the ability of banks to absorb losses, the cycle could quickly become self-fulfilling if the authorities did not intervene. A shareholder run would be the precursor to a depositor run.

Money market rates climbed as banks scrambled to fill gaping holes on their balance sheets.[51] Market commentators claimed banks were 'hoarding'. In reality, it was not fear that was stopping banks from lending to each other. The entire banking system was short of cash. Banks were paying the price for expanding their loans far and above the anaemic growth in their deposit base. Many had borrowed from abroad. By the end of March

2008, total borrowing by UK banks from abroad had risen to an astonishing £3.8 trillion, more than two-and-a-half times the annual output of the UK economy (see Figure 1.9).[52]

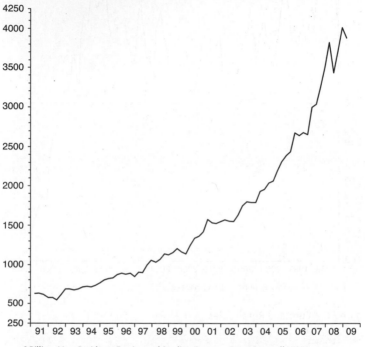

——— £ Billion, Non-Residents Foreign and Sterling Currency Deposits at all UK Monetary Institutions

Figure 1.9   UK Banks, External Liabilities

Source: Bank of England, Monetary and Financial Statistics

Mervyn King, Governor of the Bank of England, compared the UK's dependency on foreign funding to 'the reversal of capital inflows experienced by a number of emerging market economies in the 1990s'.[53] With debt-laden countries such as Hungary, Ukraine and Pakistan already turning to the International Monetary Fund, this was hardly a ringing endorsement. The unflattering comparison – from a central bank governor – sent sterling tumbling again.

The Royal Bank of Scotland (RBS), Halifax Bank of Scotland (HBOS) and Bradford & Bingley were leading the rout of UK banks. Northern Rock was not a one-off, but the first domino to topple. In the US, Washington Mutual and Lehman Brothers were the more prominent banks suffering 'shareholder runs'.[54] UBS and Fortis were just two of numerous banks across Euroland suffering from a housing market collapse that had begun in the spring of 2006, a year before the UK's bubble burst.[55]

Leaning Against the Wind

With the headline inflation rate rising, central banks ostensibly faced a dilemma. Even if the collapse of the banking system was the greater threat, they were hamstrung by nervous bond investors. Interest rate cuts may have been met by a vicious rise in bond yields. Bailing out the banks with interest rate cuts would have been interpreted by markets as a sign that central banks had gone soft on inflation.

That would have pushed lending rates – notably mortgage rates in the US – much higher. Mortgage rates in the US are critically dependent upon long-term interest rates, with many loans priced off Treasury bond yields.[56] Many corporate, consumer, student and municipal loans are also dependent upon the government bond yield.

But therein lay a major flaw with economic policy in the West. For too long, central banks have followed rather than led the market. Policymakers have been in awe of financial markets, allowing the whim of investors to dictate their response. Markets are not always right. They are frequently wrong, and it is the job of central banks to lean against the prevailing mood at critical moments. Validating their irrationality, as Alan Greenspan did in the late 1990s in response to dotcom mania, can merely add to the de-stabilising forces inherent with the laissez-faire model.

Central banks could have shaped the policy debate after the collapse of Bear Stearns, arguing forcefully that inflation was not the primary threat. They should have focused policy on stabilising house prices. By articulating the asymmetric risks, policymakers may have been able to bring down short-term interest rates without driving long-term borrowing costs higher and precipitating a collapse of investor confidence.

If the markets had not wanted to accept this premise, central banks had one obvious weapon at their disposal. They could have intervened in the market, 'attacking' long-term interest rates. They could have taken a clear stand against the prevailing wisdom.

The case for quantitative easing, a policy that directly targets long-term borrowing costs, was made in Chapter 9 of *The Credit Crunch*. It would have sent a powerful signal to rattled investors, that their inflation expectations were exaggerated and wrong. It would have shown that central banks were determined to put the stability of banks and the threat of recession first. And by 'getting ahead of the curve', they would have earned credibility.

But as the losses in the housing market started to mount, investors realised they and policymakers had miscalculated. Inflation was not the primary risk, but deflation. The battle between the two camps – a minority warning that debt deflation was the predominant threat versus a majority warning of a return to a 1970s cycle of rising prices – had been contentious, heated and at times, polemic.

In reality, the evidence of the deflation threat was overwhelming even by the early summer of 2008. Attempts to invigorate the US economy with tax rebates in the spring had failed. Wages were still being squeezed and tensions in the credit markets were starting to spill over into commodity prices.

But the central banks refused to budge. Libor, the cost of banks lending to each other in money markets, remained persistently high over the summer of 2008 (see Figure 1.10). The failure of Libor to fall in response to repeated liquidity injections from August 2007 onwards should have warned policymakers they had been wrong not to cut interest rates.[57]

Critical time was lost and share prices started to slide. The losses suffered by investors and banks in the housing market would now be compounded by steep reversals in equities, corporate bonds and countless other leveraged investments. The collapse in asset prices ran away from the authorities. They lost control.

—— $ 3-Month London Interbank Offered Rate Minus Federal Funds (Effective) – Middle Rate

Figure 1.10   US Libor Spread, July 2007 to June 2009

Source: Thomson Reuters Datastream

Lehman Brothers Crashes

Nothing symbolises this loss of control more than the demise of Lehman Brothers. It was no secret that the US investment bank had been struggling to dispose of toxic assets, to get its critical debt to leverage ratio down. Just like Northern Rock, its problems had been well-known to market participants. There had been numerous opportunities to stabilise Lehman Brothers. The Korea Development Bank had offered to inject capital that would have saved the 158-year-old Wall Street giant.[58]

The Lehman Brothers chair, Richard Fuld, had dithered, holding out for a better bid and the offer was withdrawn. Over the weekend of 13–14 September 2008, with its share price down 94 per cent that year alone, the US authorities presided over the Wall Street equivalent of a car boot sale, as Barclays and Bank of America were allowed to pick over the Lehman carcass.[59]

US Treasury Secretary Hank Paulson was unwilling to nationalise Lehman Brothers and begged the banks to deliver a rescue. By late Sunday, however, there were no offers. Realising that the stock market would cast its devastating verdict on the Monday morning, trashing the share price of the three remaining investment banks, Merrill Lynch jumped into the protective arm of Bank of America. Lehman Brothers was abandoned and left with no alternative, other than to file for bankruptcy.

Many large institutional investors had assets held in custody by Lehman Brothers. They were forced to liquidate other assets, to compensate for the estimated $44 billion of assets frozen within Lehman Brothers. Panic selling sent financial markets into a tailspin.[60]

Two vocal journalists with the *Financial Times* declared that the decision to let Lehman Brothers default was a triumph for free markets. 'What if Lehman files for bankruptcy and nothing much happens?' pondered one. 'I was pleased that Hank Paulson, the Treasury Secretary heeded my advice…and refused to rescue Lehman Brothers. Guess what? The world did not end on Monday', proclaimed the second.[61]

They would soon be proved wrong. Within hours American Insurance Group, the world's largest insurer, was spiralling towards default. Share prices in the two remaining investment banks, Goldman Sachs and Morgan Stanley, also began to slide.

In an ironic twist, John Mack, the Morgan Stanley chair, attacked short sellers for driving down the bank's share price. Hedge funds would borrow from banks, to sell shares they did not own, hoping to profit from a falling market. But Morgan Stanley was the largest lender to hedge funds. So long as the hedge funds were targeting other companies, selling their shares, Morgan Stanley had been happy to do business with them. As soon as they were focusing on one of the premier US investment banks, the howls of protest went all the way to the top.

The US administration and Federal Reserve had totally misjudged the fallout from Lehman Brothers' demise. It was indeed too big to fail and too interconnected in a web of financial market transactions. The scale of the collapse was illustrated by the bankruptcy of the Lehman Brothers subsidiary in Tokyo. With liabilities of ¥3.4 trillion or $32.4 billion, it was the largest ever bank failure in Japan, eclipsing all the bankruptcies bar one during Japan's long bear market – the demise of the insurance company, Kyoei Life.[62]

The US Treasury and Federal Reserve had been heavily criticised for rescuing Bear Stearns. That another US investment bank had slipped into trouble was proof that US officials had been too soft, fuelling moral hazard. They needed to act tough, otherwise banks would continue to take excessive risks. There would never be an end to the boom and bust cycle. The critics wanted the market to take its natural course.

But it was a failure of regulation that had allowed investment banks to take on such aggressive bets in the first place. The role of deregulation and the laissez-faire approach of governments in creating the crisis were conveniently ignored. In 2004, the Securities Exchange Commission had removed a key constraint on US investment banks, which had previously capped their debt to capital ratio at 12.[63] They would now be allowed to expand their balance sheet to much greater multiples. This so-called leverage ratio duly soared to over 30-to-1, as the investment banks increased their bets on the direction of financial markets.

Having bowed to the clamour not to intervene over Lehman Brothers, the catastrophic effects on markets from the biggest bank failure in history forced a U-turn. Less than 48 hours after Lehman Brothers had collapsed, American Insurance Group was bailed out with an injection of $85 billion and effectively nationalised.[64] But the selling continued. Morgan Stanley and Goldman Sachs were next, but if they were nationalised too, the slide in share prices across the remaining banks would accelerate. Investors would simply move on to the next bank in trouble, and there were plenty to choose from. US Treasury Secretary Hank

Paulson and Fed chair Ben Bernanke had reached the end of the road. They turned to Congress.

Another Bailout

On three sides of A4 paper, Mr Paulson demanded $700 billion to be deployed at his discretion bailing out the banks. The money would be used to remove the mortgage-backed bonds, which had caused such big losses, from the balance sheets of major banks.[65] By driving the price of these mortgage bonds higher, the US authorities would reduce the losses facing banks. They wanted to rig the market, in an attempt to get the banks lending again.

The policy was justified on the spurious grounds that the bonds were mispriced. They had supposedly plummeted in value because of a liquidity crisis, not because the underlying asset – houses – had fallen in value. In reality, the bonds had fallen so far because many homeowners who had taken out mortgages in recent years were likely to default. And the bonds were leveraged instruments. Their price would fall disproportionately in response to any given increase in the expected default rate.

Stock markets stabilised in response to Mr Paulson's plans. Finally, it seemed, the US authorities understood the severity of the crisis, and realised that many of their conventional policy tools were not working.

But the drama was not over as Congress stalled the bailout, and share prices resumed their slide.[66] Washington Mutual had finally succumbed on 25 September 2008, but it was a mere footnote amidst the turmoil and vacuum created by a dithering US administration.[67] A lack of detail in Mr Paulson's submission and the unlimited discretion sought by the US Treasury Secretary had been too much to swallow.

After more than a week of tense negotiations, the attempted rescue of banks was passed at the second attempt by Congress, and stock markets rallied again. The respite was brief – $700 billion was a lot of money, but the losses faced by banks were huge too.

And the US authorities had failed to arrest the slide in the housing market. Despite repeated injections of liquidity from the Federal Reserve, mortgage rates were not coming down. There had been no improvement in borrowing costs. Indeed, by late August the average 30-year mortgage rate was higher than levels prevailing just before the collapse of Bear Stearns.[68] On that basis alone, there was no reason to expect house prices to stop falling, not in 2009 or beyond.

Nationalisation Not Enough

The nationalisation of Freddie Mac and Fannie Mae on 7 September, the giant lenders responsible for more than half of all mortgages in the US, was supposed to have reassured investors and brought down borrowing costs. The day after they had been taken over by the US administration, financial commentators confidently proclaimed that the newly acquired official status of these two lenders would lead to lower funding costs. 'The initial reaction from the market was euphoric... holding out the prospect of lower mortgage rates that could mitigate the US housing slump', claimed the *Financial Times*.[69]

It did – for around a week – and then mortgage rates started to climb again.[70] There were lingering doubts over whether lenders to Freddie Mac and Fannie Mae really did have an explicit guarantee from the US Treasury.

But the US authorities were about to discover a hard truth about bank bailouts. Taking private sector loans and dumping them on to the taxpayer did not eliminate the risk, particularly when the debts were so large in the first place. Furthermore, most investors had in reality assumed that the debts of Freddie and Fannie would be honoured by the state in the event of default. There was no reason for borrowing costs to fall just because the lenders had been nationalised.

Indeed, the state-led rescue merely drove home to financial markets the dire outlook. Over the coming weeks, Freddie and Fannie would see their borrowing costs rise, sending mortgage rates higher.

A Bailout for UK Banks

In the UK, bank share prices were coming under renewed pressure too. The banks had been busy writing down the value of their loans, and had gone to shareholders for fresh capital in the spring. However, with house prices sliding in the US and UK, investors were starting to lose their nerve. The banks could not survive without fresh capital, but it would be impossible to go back to the market again so soon for another handout.

After much dithering, Chancellor of the Exchequer Alistair Darling announced that three of the banks – RBS, HBOS and Lloyds TSB – would be part nationalised with a capital injection of £37 billion. Overall, a total of £500 billion would be used to shore up the banking system, including liquidity injections and state guarantees.[71]

The Labour Party faithful roared their approval, as did stock market investors. Capitalism lived to breathe again – thanks to the state. For a decade, as Chancellor, Gordon Brown had presided over the most grotesque credit bubble in the country's history. But no matter. He was riding to the rescue using nothing less than old fashioned Labour-style intervention, it seemed.

In truth, the free market ideology running through the heart of the New Labour project stopped Brown and Darling from nationalising the banks properly. They insisted on a hands-off management of the banks. This was not a return to state intervention of old, but a temporary policy. Once the banks had repaid the government loans, they would be free to carry on as before.

But the banks had no incentive to bring their lending rates down. When the Bank of England belatedly cut interest rates by 1.5 per cent to 3.0 per cent on 6 November 2008 – the second reduction in just over a month – the banks were censured by the media and politicians for not passing on the benefit to borrowers.[72] Chancellor Alistair Darling summoned the chief executives of banks to Downing Street for a meeting to demand lower mortgage rates.

The government wanted it both ways. It was charging a punitive 12 per cent on preference shares acquired in exchange for part of its capital injection into RBS, HBOS and Lloyds TSB. It was trying to act tough, but the terms of the government's rescue were perverse. It would be even harder for banks to cut their lending rates, thus exacerbating the decline in lending. Not for the first time, the UK authorities seemed not to comprehend the dynamics of the crisis they had created.

The banks were also being hit by a collapse of capital markets. Nervous investors were pulling out of the commercial paper and corporate bond markets, critical sources of borrowing for large companies. Banks were also forced to support an array of other financial corporations, or quasi lenders that had depended on wholesale funding to stay in business.

Much of the so-called shadow banking system was also migrating back on to the balance sheets of major banks. It had been designed to avert the need for any capital cushion. Lending was conducted off-balance sheet in a regulatory black hole. Some was concentrated in conduits set up by banks in offshore tax havens. Other lending was funnelled through Structured Investment Vehicles or SIVs.

When the bubble burst, many of the 'assets' underpinning these lending vehicles suddenly became worthless. The banks were forced to report losses on their conduits and SIVs, exposing them to public scrutiny for the first time and obliging banks to bring the loans back on to their balance sheets.[73]

Over the summer of 2008, money supply growth surged in the UK despite a collapse in lending to households and companies.[74] The banks were squeezing individuals and business, to make room on their balance sheets for the plethora of quasi lenders that had expanded aggressively during the boom (see Figure 1.11). Many could no longer secure funding in the capital markets. These lenders could not be allowed to fail, because that would rebound on the UK banks, driving their share price lower. Many had close links to UK banks. In other cases, their failure could have led to even more forced selling of assets driving prices lower, and triggering more losses for the banks. It was easier to squeeze households and businesses (see Figure 1.12).[75]

Again the government complained. Lord Mandelson, the new Business Secretary, fretted that the lifeline for many companies

Figure 1.11   UK Bank Lending to Other Financial Institutions

Source: Bank of England

was being cut.[76] Few businesses could borrow on the capital markets. And if they did, the rates were penal. For companies that were non-investment grade – rated BB or lower by agencies such as Moody's or Standard & Poor's – the average cost of borrowing in the bond market soared to over 27 per cent. That was more than double the cost of funding prevailing prior to the collapse of Lehman Brothers. It would eventually climb above 34 per cent by early April 2009.[77] More than anything, the huge jump in borrowing costs underlined the damage inflicted by the decision to allow Lehman Brothers to default.

It was the same across Euroland where comparable rates had jumped to 26 per cent.[78] In the US, non-investment grade

Figure 1.12   UK Bank Lending to Personal Sector

Source: Bank of England

companies were also having to pay extreme rates to refinance or rollover existing debt, as rates climbed to a peak of more than 22 per cent.[79] Auto manufacturers, including General Motors and Ford, were being charged nearly 50 per cent, as they teetered on the brink of default.[80] Companies with a credit rating of BAA – the lower end of the investment grade spectrum – saw their borrowing costs in the US rise from under 6 per cent to more than 9.5 per cent.[81]

Unemployment Soars

Punitive borrowing costs spelt disaster for many workers. Companies were slashing jobs to stave off default brought on by collapsing demand and a penal rise in borrowing costs. In the US, the official but 'narrow' unemployment rate had already risen for nine consecutive months, from a 2007 low of 4.4 per cent to 6.2 per cent by September 2008, when Lehman Brothers collapsed.[82] As the catastrophic impact of the bank's failure and the doubling of borrowing costs ripped through corporate America, job losses surged. By the end of the year, the monthly job losses in the US had leapt to 681,000. That was double the losses seen at the worst point of the previous two recessions, and far worse than anything seen in the early 1980s. It was even higher than December 1974, when 602,000 were shed in the midst of the oil embargo.[83] In January 2009, nearly three quarters of a million jobs were shed.

By early June, financial markets were celebrating, as the US administration announced that monthly job losses had slowed to 'just' 345,000. But that was worse than any point in the previous two recessions. And the official jobless rate had still risen to 9.4 per cent. There was every chance that it would climb above the post-war high of 10.8 per cent set in 1982.[84]

That hardly told the full story. The official unemployment rate in the US fails to capture many who have given up looking for work. In the survey conducted by the Bureau of Labor Statistics, anyone not actively looking for a job over the preceding four weeks does not count as unemployed.

Furthermore, the collapse of capital markets in the autumn of 2008 triggered a massive rise in the number of part-time workers. By May 2009, 9.1 million Americans were working part-time, their hours cut 'due to economic circumstances'.[85]

Combining these 'marginally attached' and the 'workers on involuntary part-time' provided a more accurate picture of the deterioration in the US labour market. This so-called U6 unemployment rate had surged to 16.4 per cent by May 2009.[86] Without a radical shift in economic policy, it was destined to climb further.

The rise in unemployment in the UK was initially less pronounced, because the bursting of the housing bubble began much later. By early 2009, unemployment had nevertheless climbed above 2.2 million. February saw the biggest rise in the numbers on dole queues on record. And employment was shrinking at the fastest rate since records began in 1971.[87]

Other countries that had seen their house prices collapse were suffering. In Spain, unemployment soared in 2008. And it carried on accelerating upwards in the early months of 2009 rising to over 3.7 million and 18.1 per cent of the workforce (see Figure 1.13).[88] Determined efforts – by a Socialist government – to send immigrant workers home could not stop the relentless rise in the jobless total that was heading for 20 per cent by the summer of 2009.

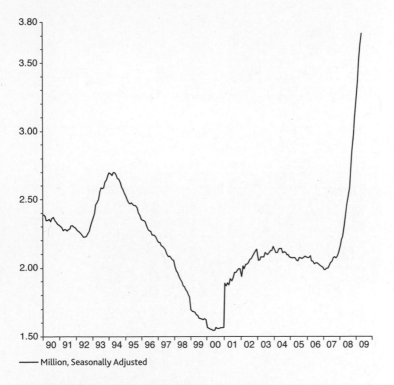

—— Million, Seasonally Adjusted

Figure 1.13   Spain Unemployment

Source: Ministerio De Economia Y Hacienda

With the European Central Bank still blinded by an out of date ideology, the potential for severe unrest was clear. Across Euroland the jobless rate had risen to 9.2 per cent by April 2009. But the unemployment rate for those aged 25 and under was more than double, a worrying 18.5 per cent. In Spain, 36.2 per cent of those under 25 were without work.[89] But by far the greatest dangers lay across Eastern Europe, the biggest victims of the credit crunch.

2
LEARNING FROM THE GREAT DEPRESSION

Once the process of asset deflation becomes entrenched, conventional policy can fail. That remains self-evident from Japan's excruciating, decade-long struggle to reverse its slump. Interest rates fell to 0.5 per cent in 1995 more than five years after the collapse in property prices had begun.[1] But that still could not stop Japan lurching from one banking crisis to another, culminating in the nationalisation of the Long Term Credit and Nippon Credit Banks in late 1998, the demise of five major life insurers between 2001 and 2003, and the failure of Resona Bank in May 2003.[2] At the time, Resona was Japan's fifth-largest bank.

Huge increases in government spending were unable to stem the slide too. Eleven emergency budgets saw the Japanese government's debt burden soar from 65 per cent of GDP in 1990 to a calamitous 175 per cent of GDP 15 years later. That was far higher than any other industrialised country.[3] No matter how hard the Japanese authorities tried, traditional policy weapons never worked. Japan was subsumed in a Fisher-style debt trap.[4]

The banking crises of 2008 were no different, it seemed. Interest rates were already down to 2.0 per cent in the US when the stock market began to tumble in the autumn. In response to a precipitous decline in share prices, the Federal Reserve cut its key lending rate twice in October to 1 per cent, and then down to virtually zero on 16 December.

But timing is critical with monetary policy. And the first reduction in interest rates in the US did not materialise until two years after signs of a reversal in property prices had emerged in the autumn of 2005.[5] Even then, the Federal Reserve only

43

cut in response to a crisis, never getting ahead of events. By the end of 2008, short-term interest rates had come up against the 'zero bound'. They could hardly go any lower, and yet property prices were still spiralling down, driving the economy deeper into recession.[6] The Fed had mistimed spectacularly.

That left a number of weapons, including one option deployed in the US in April 1932 – the purchase of Treasury bonds (Treasuries) or government debt. The policy was then labelled *large-scale open market purchases* because it involved a central bank entering the market and buying government debt, or bonds. Latterly, it was labelled quantitative easing, after a similar policy was adopted by Japan in 2001. Because bond prices are inversely related to yields, buying Treasuries can drive yields or long-term interest rates down.

This can, in turn, push mortgage rates lower. In the US, as we have already seen, most mortgage rates are set in relation to the Treasury bond yield. Treasury yields effectively act as the 'risk-free' interest rate and a baseline for all borrowing costs, since it is assumed that governments will not default.

Governments have defaulted in the past, particularly when they have borrowed heavily from abroad. The Argentine government defaulted on $95 billion of debt in December 2001, the largest ever sovereign default.[7] Since successive US administrations have in recent years financed much of their debt from abroad, it was understandable that investors might fret over the possibility of a US government default.[8]

A Capital Crunch

Nevertheless, the US government is deemed the least risky counterparty or option for investors. For that reason, Treasury bond yields still underpin all other credit costs, including mortgage rates and corporate bond yields. As Figures 2.1 and 2.2 show, the latter are critical for determining both the borrowing costs and availability of credit for many companies.[9]

The surge in yields on these bonds had decimated the capital base of banks during the early 1930s. Many had accumulated a

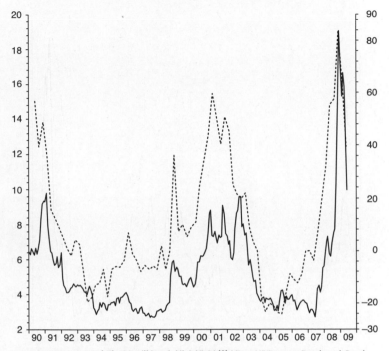

Figure 2.1   US Corporate Bond Spreads and Banks Tightening Credit

Source: Thomson Reuters Datastream and Federal Reserve

large exposure to corporate bonds during the boom of the late 1920s. As companies raced to expand, they issued bonds to fund their growth. But as the risk of these companies defaulting grew during the long slump, the price on these bonds fell, pushing the yield up.

Lower bond prices meant deep losses for the banks.[10] Indeed, as the yields rose, banks were forced to dump their bonds, causing even bigger losses among banks and more forced liquidation. As banks collapsed, there was less credit available, the economy deteriorated, more companies went bust and unemployment

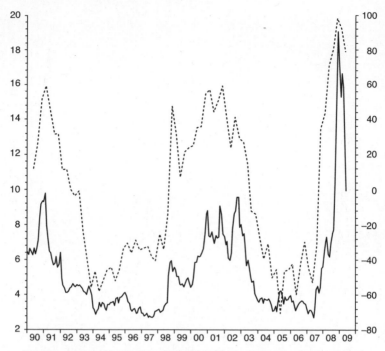

——— US Corporate Bond, The Merrill Lynch High Yield ($) Minus US Treasury Benchmark Bond, 10 Year Redemption Yield

— — Net %, C&I (Commercial and Industrial) Loan Survey – Large and Medium Firms, Banks Increase Rate/Cost of Funds Spread (RH Scale)

Figure 2.2   US Corporate Bond Spreads and Banks Increasing Rate/Cost of Funds Spread

Source: Thomson Reuters Datastream and Federal Reserve

soared. Corporate bond prices fell further. It was a vicious circle and a classic market failure. Attempts by individual banks to preserve capital were threatening to bring all of them down.

The banking system was in meltdown. The only way out of the mire was for the Federal Reserve to intervene in the market and reverse the rise in corporate borrowing costs to stop companies defaulting. However, it was not done through the purchase of corporate bonds. Under heavy Congressional pressure, the Federal Reserve started buying Treasuries through a programme of open market purchases.

There was nothing particularly radical about this policy. It had become an accepted instrument for central banks to use during periods of distress. Indeed, at the time, it was widely regarded as 'the most potent monetary tool' in the Federal Reserve's kit.[11]

There was an accepted logic behind the Federal Reserve's actions. By pushing down the so-called risk-free rate, it let the market decide which companies should be refinanced at lower rates. The market would drive down corporate borrowing costs. If the Federal Reserve intervened in the corporate bond market, it would have been picking winners and losers, fostering moral hazard. By driving this baseline for all borrowing costs lower, the Federal Reserve would still allow the market to decide which companies would survive.

Within a month, this concerted attempt to drive down the yield on government bonds started to lower the yield on corporate

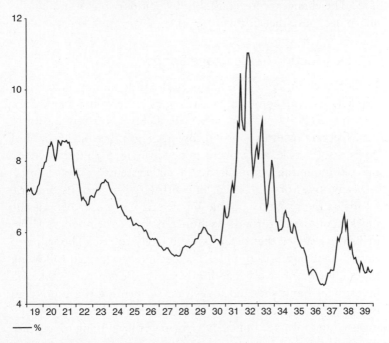

Figure 2.3   Corporate Bond Yields, 1919 to 1939

Source: Moody's Seasoned Corporate Bond Yield, BAA

bonds. The average yield on corporate bonds for companies with a rating of BAA peaked at 11.6 per cent in May 1932. Over the summer of that year, yields fell steadily, touching 7.6 per cent in September (see Figure 2.3).[12]

The policy was not pursued anywhere near aggressively enough. The drop in corporate borrowing costs remained inadequate, because the Fed had been far from united in its pursuit of lower government bond yields.

But in so much that it was tried, it stopped the rot. And this important episode showed that quantitative easing was a critical weapon in the battle against debt deflation. It helped to turn the tide in 1932. Money supply still tumbled in the early months of 1933, but the impact of quantitative easing could be seen over the summer of 1932. The decline in bank deposits reached a trough in July that year and money supply hit an interim low two months later. The changes were small, but by comparison with the prior sharp declines, 'the shift was major'.[13]

The Destruction of Mortgage Bonds

In today's credit crunch, it has been the slide in mortgage bonds – residential and commercial – that has undermined banks, not just in the US but across the world. These bonds were sold to unsuspecting investors abroad. By tapping into a bigger pool of investors, the risks were meant to be 'diversified', but they ended up contaminating a globalised financial system.[14]

Many investors had been left with large portfolios of these bonds as the property bubble burst, unable to sell them as the market suddenly turned. As house prices continued to slide, investors realised that defaults were likely to rise. The value of these bonds began to tumble. The decline accelerated following the implosion of two hedge funds run by Bear Stearns. The US investment bank shocked investors, confirming the funds had lost nearly all of their money.[15] The hedge funds had been heavily invested in mortgage bonds, borrowing or leveraging to increase potential returns.

A year later, following the collapse of Bear Stearns, the slide in mortgage bonds intensified. Many of the bonds fell to less than 10 per cent of their original issue price. Even AAA bonds, supposedly safe but routinely packed with sub-prime loans, fell precipitously. By early 2009, some mortgage bonds had fallen 97 per cent from their peak. AAA bonds had lost more than three quarters of their value in a number of cases.[16]

Table 2.1   Markit ABX.HE closing prices

Index	High	Low	%change
ABX.HE.AAA.07-2	99.33	23.1	–76.74
ABX.HE.AA.07-2	97.00	3.94	–95.93
ABX.HE.A.07-2	81.94	2.97	–96.37
ABX.HE.BBB.07-2	56.61	2.89	–94.89
ABX.HE.AAA.07-1	100.09	23.25	–76.77
ABX.HE.AA.07-1	100.09	2.86	–97.14
ABX.HE.A.07-1	100.01	2.33	–97.67
ABX.HE.BBB.07-1	98.35	2.19	–97.77
ABX.HE.AAA.06-2	100.12	29.00	–71.03
ABX.HE.AA.06-2	100.12	7.60	–92.41
ABX.HE.A.06-2	100.12	3.53	–96.47
ABX.HE.BBB.06-2	100.59	2.29	–97.72
ABX.HE.AAA.06-1	100.38	59.75	–40.47
ABX.HE.AA.06-1	100.73	16.13	–83.99
ABX.HE.A.06-1	100.51	7.72	–92.32
ABX.HE.BBB.06-1	101.20	3.95	–96.10

Source: Markit, www.markit.com/en/products/data/indices/structured-finance-indices/abx/abx-prices.page?,

Mortgage bonds fulfilled the same destructive role as corporate bonds during the early years of the Great Depression. They decimated the capital bases of banks. In both cases the authorities needed to intervene to break the vicious cycle, where liquidation of portfolios was triggering more forced selling. Otherwise, the entire banking system might collapse.

Relapse in 1933

The policy of large-scale open market purchases or quantitative easing adopted in 1932 did not stop more banks failing. During the final months of that year, a large number of banks collapsed in 'the Midwest and Far West', while 'there was a sharp spurt in January [1933] involving a wider area'.[17]

The decision to raise interest rates to defend the dollar in one last desperate attempt to prevent a collapse of the Gold Standard backfired too. The UK government's decision to abandon the Gold Standard in September 1931 was beginning to take its toll. The subsequent decline in sterling led the Federal Reserve to raise interest rates even as the economy contracted. Interest rates went up in the autumn of 1931 and again in early 1933.[18] However, the crisis in early 1933 'was even more serious than in September 1931 because of all that had gone before... the panic was far more widespread'.[19]

An important cause of this was 'the drastically weakened capital position of the commercial banks, which had made them vulnerable to even minor drains of funds'. Furthermore, 'The recorded capital figures were widely recognized as overstating the available capital, because assets were being carried on the books at a value higher than their market value.'[20]

This suggests that calls for banks to be allowed to shift from 'mark-to-market' accounting during the credit crunch of 2007 and 2008, were misplaced. Numerous financial commentators – and politicians – claimed that the run on banks might have been avoided if they had not been obliged to mark assets down to the prevailing market price. The 1930s showed otherwise.[21]

That did not stop a shift in policy that helped banks to massage their profit numbers in the early months of 2009, with the Obama administration's complicit approval. Wells Fargo managed to 'hoodwink' investors, by marking its assets higher by $4.4 billion under a change in accounting rules, sparking a rally in share prices that was in turn cited as proof of 'economic recovery'.[22]

The vulnerability of banks during the 1933 run also underlined the folly of failing to deliver more aggressive quantitative easing *a priori*. More substantive open market purchases in 1932 extending over a longer period 'would have improved the capital position [of banks] by raising market values'.[23]

A Disunited Fed

But the Federal Reserve had been a reluctant convert to quantitative easing. Indeed, there were deep schisms within the Fed that severely hampered the operation of monetary policy, and contributed hugely to a deepening of the economic contraction. The Fed was not, and is still not, a single central bank like the Bank of England, but a composition of regional reserve banks. At the time of the stock market crash in 1929, policy decisions were carried out by the Open Market Investment Committee. This was superseded by the Open Market Policy Conference in March 1930.[24] Both were similar to the Federal Open Market Committee (FOMC), which today serves as the body for policy-making decisions. As with the FOMC, governors from the regional or Federal Reserve banks had a vote on monetary policy matters.

One of these reserve banks was the New York Fed. Its governor George Harrison was also chair of the Open Market Investment Committee and the Open Market Policy Conference. After share prices collapsed in October 1929, the New York Bank had few doubts about the steps that needed to be taken. It purchased $160 million of government securities during the final months of 1929.[25] This was the first attempt to ameliorate the downturn through quantitative easing. Interest rates were also cut swiftly.[26]

But other members of the Open Market Investment Committee were against these open market purchases. There was resentment that the New York Fed had acted without consent, even though the bonds had been bought for the bank's own account. There was a power struggle within an organisation facing its first big test since its creation in 1913.

Repeated attempts by the New York Fed to pursue a more expansionary monetary policy were rejected by other members of the newly formed Open Market Policy Conference. In July 1930, three months before the first banking crisis erupted, Mr Harrison wrote a long letter to all governors of the other Federal Reserve banks arguing the case for more quantitative easing, pleading that the 'Federal Reserve System do everything possible and within its power to facilitate a recovery of business'.[27] Harrison acknowledged 'there may be no definite assurance that open market operations in government securities will of themselves promote any immediate recovery'. However, there was clearly no 'appreciable harm' in trying. The 'seriousness of the present depression is so great as to justify taking every possible step to facilitate improvement'.[28] The warning was ignored.

In response to Harrison's letter, the governor of the Chicago Fed, James McDougal, noted there was already an 'abundance' of liquidity. There was a danger that 'speculation might easily arise in some other direction'.[29] Mr McDougal even pushed for a reversal of the modest quantitative easing authorised at the previous meeting.

Another opponent of the New York Fed was John Calkins, head of the San Francisco Federal Reserve Bank. He argued that a recovery would not 'be accelerated by making credit cheaper', and urged the Open Market Policy Conference to wait for a more 'opportune moment' to take action.[30] However, such a moment would surely arrive through inaction.

Lynn Talley of the Dallas Federal Reserve Bank was also against 'artificial methods' to reverse the effects of stock market speculation that had precipitated the crash. It is 'quite impossible to bring the patient back to life through the use of artificial respiration or injections of adrenalin', declared Mr Talley.[31]

Further objections to quantitative easing came from W.B. Geery, the head of the Minneapolis Reserve Bank. He was worried about the 'danger of stimulating financing'. Paradoxically, he fretted over the prospect of 'still more overproduction', while worrying about the effects of easier finance in promoting consumption.[32]

And the Philadelphia Fed Reserve chief, George Norris, warned against 'attempting to depress still further the abnormally low interest rates now prevailing'. He added, 'We have been putting out credit in a period of depression, when it is not wanted, and could not be used, and will have to withdraw credit when it is wanted and can be used.'[33]

This became a familiar excuse many years later. In response to the belated introduction of quantitative easing in 2009, policymakers spent much time fretting over how and when the policy would be reversed, before it had been given a chance to work.[34]

Parochialism

The contrast between the New York Fed and other Reserve Banks was due to 'extraordinary differences...in the level of sophistication and understanding about monetary matters'. In part, this reflected the role of New York as the home of the country's money market, which had given the New York Fed a 'sensitive recognition of the effects of monetary policy actions'. By contrast, the regional reserve banks had been largely concerned with 'local and regional matters'.[35] And they were inclined to view intervention as a sop to over-speculation.

Having initially tried to support the economy through quantitative easing, the Federal Reserve's policy became highly restrictive from December 1929. During the summer of 1930, the governor of the New York Fed pleaded for more direct action, to no avail. He was not alone. Another New York official warned that 'this deflation should now be aggressively combated by additional purchases of Government securities', but again he was ignored.[36]

But 1931 was little better. The collapse of the Bank of United States in December 1930 had forced the New York Fed to intervene on its own account, as it had in late 1929.[37] Other Federal Reserve Banks defiantly refused to support New York. Indeed, the Open Market Policy Conference voted in January 1931 to tighten policy, reversing the modest quantitative easing that had taken place.

Eugene Meyer, governor of the Federal Reserve Board, was aghast and warned of political repercussions, warning that 'The [Federal] Reserve System has been accused in a number of quarters of pursuing a deflationary policy in the past year, and a sale of government securities at this time is likely to draw fire.'[38]

There was a sense of inevitability over the next banking crisis when it erupted in March 1931. A month later, the governor of the New York Fed proposed that the Federal Reserve buy $100 million of government securities in a belated attempt to ease this latest crisis. The resolution was passed 'with four reluctant supporters'.[39] And it was barely implemented. The buying did not begin until after a further meeting held on 22 June and then stopped on 16 July, with only $30 million of securities purchased.[40]

On 11 August 1931, Harrison pressed for more authorisation, this time to buy $300 million of government securities. Again, he was overruled, and had to settle for a limit of $120 million.[41] That, claimed one senior Fed official agitating for stronger action, was an 'ineffective amount'.[42]

By early 1932, New York Bank officials were once again pushing for radical intervention, and the Open Market Policy Conference was authorised to conduct $200 million of open market purchases 'if necessary'.[43] The Fed failed even to exploit this limited agreement. Monetary policy remained too tight and the economy continued to slide deeper into depression.

An exasperated Congress began to exert pressure on the Fed, threatening 'radical financial legislation'.[44] Treasury Secretary Ogden Mills spoke for the Hoover administration when he declared that the lack of action was 'almost inconceivable and almost unforgivable'. He pleaded for the policy options available to the Fed to 'be put to work on a scale commensurate with the existing emergency'.[45]

Turning the Tide, Reflation Begins

Eventually, the Fed voted on 12 April 1932 to expand quantitative easing. It would purchase $500 million of government securities, in addition to the unexpired authority agreed at the previous meeting. The purchases were to be made 'as rapidly as practicable'.[46] This last provision was inserted after Harrison had warned that 'he was scheduled to testify the next day before a subcommittee of the House on a bill that in effect would have directed the Reserve system to purchase [government securities or Treasuries] in the open market until wholesale prices had risen to their 1926 level'.[47]

At its next monthly meeting, the Fed voted to expand the open market purchases by a further $500 million, but there were two dissenting voices – the Chicago and Boston Federal Reserve Banks. The Open Market Policy Conference also debated slowing the pace of buying. Over the five weeks since the previous meeting, the Fed had been buying government securities at the rate of $100 million per week. Harrison was furious, warning that 'The temper of Congress is not improving.'[48]

The full authority agreed at the May meeting was utilised, and by the end of June the Fed had bought $1,000 million of government securities. But again, Chicago and Boston tried to stop quantitative easing. One official of the New York Fed complained bitterly, warning that the policy action to date had merely stopped the effects of a contraction in credit availability. The Fed had not yet gone far enough to 'stimulate an expansion of credit' to reflate the economy.[49] The New York official added, to stop now 'would be a ridiculous thing to do. We shall have no policy left if we do this.'[50] The Fed had reached a point where it was now able to apply the pressure quantitative easing was 'designed to produce'. The Fed was merely 'half way through' its programme.[51]

The head of the Chicago Fed countered, declaring he could 'not see what the purchases have done anyway'. The Boston Fed chief's argument was even more disingenuous. Further bank failures were inevitable, governor Young warned, and that would lead to more borrowing from the Fed. Therefore, he concluded, 'We are wasting our resources buying government securities.'[52]

That the purchase of government securities was meant to forestall bank failures was completely lost on Young. The deputy chair of the New York Fed travelled to Illinois, in an attempt to persuade the directors of the Chicago Fed to change their mind, but he failed.

Boston and Chicago were in the minority, but their dissents had a significant influence. Governor Harrison was worried that proceeding without their support would compromise the unity of the Federal Reserve. And at its next monthly meeting on 14

July 1932, the Fed decided to purchase government securities at a miserly $5 million to $15 million a week.[53] That was not restrictive enough for the Boston or Chicago Feds, who were joined by the Richmond Fed in voting against the resolution. Two days after the meeting, Congress adjourned. Freed from political pressure, the Fed conducted open market purchases at the minimum level consistent with the July compromise, buying a mere $30 million of government securities. And from 10 August until the end of 1932, monetary policy went neutral. Boston and Chicago refused to participate in any further efforts to support the economy and the head of New York 'was unwilling to proceed on his own'.[54]

By early January 1933, the Fed was coming under pressure again to relent. But the US central bank proceeded instead to vote for a tightening of policy at its 4 January meeting, reducing open market purchases by $125 million, despite opposition from Treasury officials.[55] Having stabilised the economy during the summer of 1932, the Fed was reversing tack. Yet another banking crisis loomed.

During February, the Fed did not even meet. Harrison had given up trying to forge a consensus. Each Reserve Bank conducted individual actions to stem the gathering crisis. That merely added to the 'general atmosphere of panic'.[56] The Federal Reserve had fallen into disarray and the banking system imploded.

The 'Final' Banking Crisis

The newly inaugurated President Roosevelt was forced to proclaim a nationwide bank holiday from 6–9 March.[57] The Emergency Banking Act of 1933 allowed banks to be reopened on a 'restricted' basis. Under previous laws, these banks would have been placed in receivership and liquidated. In a radio address on 12 March, the President announced a programme for reopening the banks. But over 2,000 out of 17,800 remained closed for good.[58]

The newly created Reconstruction Finance Corporation (RFC) played a crucial role in the restoration of the banking system. It invested $1 billion of taxpayers' money into 6,139 banks, equal to a third of the capital of all banks in 1933. The RFC also made loans totalling $2 billion.[59] It was an aggressive programme of assistance, often seen as the critical factor in turning the tide. Without it, the banking crisis would undoubtedly have continued. However, it cannot be separated from the impetus provided by monetary policy. The Federal Reserve could and should have done so much more but it was pulling the levers, if reluctantly. Reconstruction of the banks would not have succeeded without the requisite monetary action. Unless there is sufficient monetary stimulus injected into the economy *a priori*, the deflationary shock from bank failures, as assets are sold at knock-down prices, can trigger further bankruptcies and accelerate the economic decline.

The Savings and Loan crisis in the US during the early 1990s underlines the point. A total of 745 savings and loan associations – equivalent to UK building societies – were closed down at a cost of $124.6 billion to the taxpayer.[60] This episode has wrongly been cited as proof that aggressive restructuring and the closure of failing institutions are sufficient steps towards reflation. The rapid drop in borrowing costs that accompanied the debt write-offs in the early 1990s is often ignored. Without this, a full economic recovery would not have been possible.[61]

Extending Reflation

After November 1933, the Fed resisted any further extensive purchases, with officials claiming that the banks were awash with reserves.[62] Nevertheless, the increase in government securities held by the Federal Reserve during 1933 was still substantial.[63]

And in 1934, the US Treasury continued to push for more aggressive monetary action. The size of the Federal Reserve's balance sheet did not change, but there was a dramatic shift in its composition. The Fed sold short-term bonds and bought longer-dated Treasuries. The objective was to drive the long-term interest rate down.[64]

Selling the short-dated bonds did not raise interest rates. The borrowing cost on these bonds – Treasury certificates – was pegged at ultra low levels by the Fed's discount rate. However, by shifting the resources to longer-term bonds with much higher rates and driving them down instead, the Fed was able to reduce borrowing costs more effectively.

This was precisely the recommendation of Keynes, who had been a strong advocate of open market purchases. In a letter addressed to President Roosevelt and published in the *New York Times* on 31 December 1933, Keynes argued that there was 'no reason why you should not reduce the rate of interest on your long-term government bonds to 2½ per cent or less, with favourable repercussions on the whole bond market, if only the Federal Reserve System would replace its present holdings of short-dated Treasury issues by purchasing long-dated issues in exchange'.[65]

A letter from one influential US journalist to Keynes seemed to confirm the impact of the UK economist on US policy at this crucial moment:[66]

> I don't know whether you realise how great an effect that letter had, but I am told that it was chiefly responsible for the policy which the Treasury is now quietly but effectively pursuing of purchasing long-term Government bonds with a view to making a strong bond market and to reducing the long term rate of interest.[67]

The Recovery Takes Hold

And so the cost of borrowing fell, the pace of bankruptcies slowed and the recovery in the economy gained traction. Manufacturing output bottomed in 1932, having shrunk 47.8 per cent in three years. It clawed back a sixth of the loss in 1933. From this perspective, the recovery was comparatively swift. However, such was the scale of the contraction it was not until December 1936 that output had returned to the levels seen at the peak of 1929.[68]

In broader terms, national income did not bottom until 1933, having collapsed by 30.5 per cent in real terms over four years. As prices had tumbled too, the drop in nominal terms was an astonishing 46.1 per cent.[69]

The precise timing of the bottom in the US economy is a matter of debate. The GDP data suggest that the recovery did not really begin until after the final banking panic. The manufacturing numbers suggest there was already some recovery underway in 1932 in response to the monetary easing witnessed that year.

There is evidence to support both cases. Manufacturing output did hit bottom following the shift in Fed policy from April 1932, reaching a low three months later. But after the open market purchases stopped, the recovery stalled. As more banks failed, output tumbled again, nearly revisiting the lows of 1932 before turning up again. Thus, although there was a renewed dip, July 1932 marks the trough of the Great Depression (see Figure 2.4).[70]

Similarly, the decline in GDP in annual terms during 1933 was mild compared with the falls witnessed earlier in the first three years of the slump. In real terms, GDP dropped by just 1.9 per

——— Index, 2002=100

Figure 2.4   US Manufacturing Production, 1919 to 1939

Source: Federal Reserve

cent. But it had fallen 9.9 per cent in 1930, 7.7 per cent in 1931 and 14.8 per cent in 1932.[71] The GDP data suggest that policy was starting to work in 1932, although it was clearly insufficient, as evident from the banking turmoil in early 1933.

Pulling the Trigger Too Soon

From 1934 onwards, however, some Fed officials were beginning to fret over the risks of running a 'loose' monetary policy.[72] Banks were awash with excess reserves, but only because they wanted the extra cushion this afforded after the tumult of recent years.[73]

And while the economy was recovering, the fall in unemployment was slow. The jobless rate was still 14.3 per cent in 1937.[74] Commodity prices were bouncing back after the sharp declines witnessed during the early years of the depression. That did not stop the Federal Reserve panicking that its policy had engineered too much reflation. It prematurely turned the screw, with the first of three quick increases in bank reserve requirements, beginning in August 1936.

This aggressive tightening of monetary policy sent the economy spiralling back into recession.[75] The persistently high jobless rate showed the economy had failed to make a full recovery. The depth of the downturn in the early 1930s also implied there was little chance of inflation 'pressures' becoming embedded. Commodity prices were rising, but wages had only been supported by the New Deal.[76] Despite a determined rearguard action by organised labour and some notable victories, there had been insufficient change in the balance of power between capital and labour.

As the higher reserve requirements started to bite, the underlying weakness in wages accelerated the slump.[77] The jobless rate leapt to 19.1 per cent in 1938.[78] The economy had simply not been strong enough to withstand such a severe jolt. The failure to distinguish between the weakness of wages and rising commodity prices was a mistake the Federal Reserve was to repeat in 2008 following the collapse of the investment bank Bear Stearns.

A full economic recovery did not ultimately materialise until the onset of the Second World War. The outbreak of hostilities in Western Europe saw demand for military goods rise in the US, bringing the jobless rate down to 9.9 per cent in 1941. The Japanese attack on Pearl Harbor was then the trigger for full-scale militarisation. The jobless rate dropped finally to a low of 1.2 per cent in 1944.[79]

But the use of the Federal Reserve to fund the war effort holds important lessons. It was nothing less than large-scale quantitative easing. Government spending nearly tripled between 1941 and 1942, and then rose a further 50 per cent in the following year. Tax receipts lagged, so the budget deficit exploded to unprecedented levels – just short of 30 per cent of national income.[80]

This huge increase in defence spending was financed by the Federal Reserve buying government securities.[81] The Federal Reserve's holdings of government debt soared more than tenfold, from $2.3 billion in 1941 to $24.3 billion four years later.[82] After the war ended, the factories shifted back to producing consumer goods and aggressive quantitative easing came to an end.

Reflation in the UK

The policy of driving down long-term interest rates was also critical in securing a turnaround in the UK during the early 1930s. Again, the economic recovery was far from robust. The slump had been going on for so much longer, courtesy of Winston Churchill's decision as Chancellor of the Exchequer to take the country back on to the Gold Standard in April 1925.[83] Furthermore, investment had been held back by a secular decline in profits, which was apparent even before 1914.[84]

Keynes had warned that persevering with an overvalued exchange rate would require punitive interest rates, and that unemployment would remain high for the rest of the decade. Within a year, the jobless rate had climbed back above 14 per cent.[85]

However, Keynes was also influential in securing the 'cheap-money policy' that saw the UK finally embark on the road to recovery. Freed from the straitjacket of the gold standard, which the UK abandoned in September 1931, the Bank rate – the Bank of England's key lending rate – was cut from 6 to 5 per cent. Further cuts soon followed down to 2 per cent.[86]

But Keynes's primary concern was driving the long-term interest rate down. And in July 1932, a conversion of the war debt from 5 to 3½ per cent set the seal on the dramatic shift to 'cheap money'.[87]

Whether the original policy shift was proposed by Keynes or by Bank of England officials has been the subject of debate. There was a precedent for conversions. Between 1887 and 1889, the government converted Consols (a type of Government debt or gilts) twice from 3 to 2¾ per cent, and then to 2½ per cent.[88]

Either way, Keynes had 'certainly offered advice and presumed that such an operation would take place'.[89] He had called for such a shift on 16 November 1931 and when it materialised, he applauded the move. 'A reduction of the long-term rate of interest to a low level is probably the most necessary of all measures if we are to escape from the slump and secure a lasting revival of enterprise', Keynes declared. He added: 'The successful conversion of the War Loan to a 3½ per cent basis is, therefore, a constructive measure of the very first importance. For it represents a direct attack upon the long-term rate, much more effective in present circumstances than the indirect attack of cheap short-term money – useful and necessary though the latter is.'[90]

Lower borrowing costs played an important role in driving house building during the 1930s. Quantitative easing and rock-bottom gilt yields were instrumental in enabling building societies to fund a programme of extensive regeneration.[91] Indeed, not a single building society failed during that decade, in marked contrast to the Labour government's dismal record, with nine current or former building societies collapsing during the credit crunch from 2007 onwards.[92]

3
POLICY MISTAKES IN THE 2008/09 BEAR MARKET

This overview of the policy measures implemented during the 1930s and 1940s is important because it provides a benchmark to gauge the ineffectiveness of central banks during the recent credit crunch. There are many parallels between the economic collapse of 2008 and the depression of the early 1930s. Both were amplified by policy mistakes.

The economic contraction from late 1929 onwards was aggravated by a failure of the Federal Reserve to take more aggressive monetary action. As we have seen, there were endless arguments and debates over how far to push quantitative easing in the US. When finally – under Congressional pressure – the Fed did respond, the economy stabilised. Even then, the Fed could have done so much more.

Adherence to the Gold Standard through the first three-and-a-half years of the depression has been widely touted as a major cause of the severe economic contraction. Interest rates did rise to defend the dollar on two separate occasions. But it would have been possible for the Federal Reserve to offset the deflationary impact by driving long-term interest rates lower through quantitative easing.[1]

And the US government could have abandoned the Gold Standard earlier. Britain left in September 1931 because the deflationary costs were too much. But the US stuck to its guns, until finally under President Roosevelt, the costs were deemed unbearable too. The US authorities had a chance to pursue a more reflationary policy much earlier, but chose not to.

While many countries became embroiled in the Great Depression, the global dimension to the 2008 credit crunch was arguably as large, if not bigger. The trade imbalances were certainly greater, while the net capital flows into many of these countries were even more extreme.[2]

The Gold Standard may have been a (voluntary) straightjacket for countries in the 1920s and early 1930s, limiting their policy response. But it did ensure countries were not able to run up huge trade deficits, fuelling an excessive dependency on capital inflows. The Gold Standard was a constraint, albeit a flawed one, badly lacking in today's brave new world of globalisation. The Gold Standard was designed to prevent the very destabilising forces that have amplified the fallout from today's credit bubble.

As in the early 1930s, there were weapons at the disposal of central banks that could have mitigated much of the damage as the credit crunch ripped through the world economy in 2008. But again, the policymakers misjudged the scale of the crisis. Similarly, the Federal Reserve was found wanting during the early stages of the current housing debacle, notably in 2007, in almost identical circumstances to those prevailing in 1930 and 1931. Hundreds of mortgage lenders defaulted from late 2006 onwards without the Fed taking offsetting monetary action. The point was underlined by the collapse of Lehman Brothers. The neglect of the banking system was a critical factor in accelerating the depression during the early 1930s. Allowing a major US investment bank to default in September 2008 was surely a comparable mistake.

For much of 2008, the Fed stuck rigidly to a programme of liquidity injections, refusing to sanction a more direct 1930s-style policy that might have mitigated some of the damage. However, once house prices start to slide, injecting liquidity is not a sufficient condition for a recovery. That was a critical lesson of the 1930s. Only after the Federal Reserve had aggressively driven down all borrowing costs to relieve debtors did the tide begin to turn in 1932.

Preventing Depression

The slide into recession in 2008 was not inevitable. It is quite possible to see how different policies and a quicker response would have mitigated much of the damage seen from the credit crunch.

When *Solutions to a Liquidity Trap* was published by GFC Economics in June 2003, it was shown that quicker cuts in interest rates would have prevented Japan from slipping into a seemingly interminable bear market.[3] It would have stopped Japan from becoming engulfed in deflation. These conclusions were derived from retrospective econometric simulations.

The results of such exercises are far from foolproof and depend significantly on the model being representative of the underlying economy. No model can hope to accurately replicate the real economy, since this depends on millions of decisions being made on a daily basis.

Nevertheless, in Japan's case, the retrospective simulations were so striking that it is hard to ignore their conclusions. Policy would not have needed to be much more proactive to have avoided the cataclysmic events of the late 1990s and the multiple banking failures.

A similar conclusion can be drawn for the US, UK and Euroland today. The optimal strategy would have been for central banks to deliver quicker rate cuts from mid 2007 onwards.[4]

Getting the timing and scale of rate cuts right is self-evidently critical. If central banks jump the gun and ease too soon, the cycle of borrowing could resume, with damaging long-term effects for the stability of the economy. Going too soon is fraught with risks.

Nevertheless, cutting interest rates more aggressively from the middle of 2007 onwards, when there had already been huge problems in the US among mortgage lenders, may well have pre-empted a further deterioration in the housing market. It might have prevented bigger declines in property prices from looping back into a deeper withdrawal of credit. And it may have forestalled some of the catastrophic banking failures of 2008.

Getting Policy Wrong

Japan's experience during its long period of economic stagnation has provided clear insights into the costs of failing to adopt a radical monetary policy during a debt crisis. Timing has always been the key. Cutting short-term interest rates to virtually zero in 1995 failed because *a priori* property deflation was allowed to accelerate too far. The collapse of the housing markets caused central banks and governments to lose control.

Left to their own devices within the private sector, there is always a risk that attempts by banks to rebuild capital ratios and repair balance sheets will drive asset values down more quickly. A bank may believe that foreclosing early on a borrower in arrears will protect itself against the potential for greater losses further down the line. But with all banks engaged in this race against time, the tactic is collectively self-defeating. When deflation becomes endemic, there is potential for systemic or market failure.

That point is reached when interest rates reach zero. If property prices are still sliding, the real cost of borrowing starts to rise. And there is nothing central banks can do – interest rates cannot go negative, not on a sustained and meaningful basis.[5] Internal Federal Reserve research concluded in the spring of 2009 that interest rates needed to be set at *minus* 5 per cent when taking into account the sharply rising unemployment rate and falling inflation.[6] Self-evidently, that was not possible.

This zero bound is a widely recognised constraint for short-term interest rates, but it is also a problem for long-term borrowing costs. We have yet to see an industrialised country unable to reduce long-term interest rates far enough to, at least, partially reverse a slump. In the US (1932), UK (1932) and Japan (2001), cutting long-term interest rates and thus mortgage rates aggressively did eventually 'secure' a recovery. It may have been patchy in the first two, and in Japan's case, there were other coincident forces that drove the turnaround.[7] Nevertheless, there were monetary options available and they were used.

This is where the current crisis could yet prove more intractable. It is not clear whether central banks will be able to reverse the economic slump simply by driving long-term interest rates lower. In the US, in particular, the slide in house prices has gathered such momentum that banks have remained under pressure to keep their lending rates high. Furthermore, the slump in the housing market and huge rise in unemployment started to feed into a collapse in commercial property in early 2009. That may yet trigger further deep losses for banks.[8]

The zero bound could, therefore, prove an effective constraint for long-term rates too. Treasury yields could conceivably be pushed down to very low levels, and still not stabilise both property markets or succeed in reflating the economy. The policy worked in the early 1930s but one cannot assume that it will always succeed. The longer it is left, the more diluted will be its impact, as the rate of property deflation accelerates.

The problem can be seen through the prism of the Irving Fisher debt deflation theory. In 1932, Fisher argued that rising real borrowing costs were an important stage in the slide towards a debt trap and occurs when attempts to write-off bad debts perversely creates more problem loans, not fewer. Attempts to dispose of non-performing loans result in more deflation and economic contraction causing real borrowing costs to rise. Real debts climb and balance sheets deteriorate. There seems to be no way out of the slump.[9]

Wrong Move

After Bear Stearns collapsed in March 2008, the Federal Reserve switched to a policy of liquidity injections. There was a liquidity crisis, but critically borrowing costs were too high. It was the high borrowing costs that were responsible for the liquidity problems. Liquidity was evaporating at regular intervals because creditors feared debtors would become insolvent. And debtors were failing because their borrowing costs were not coming down quickly enough as asset prices tumbled.

Instead of cutting interest rates more aggressively, the Federal Reserve and other central banks injected vast sums of liquidity into the money markets. They assumed that the money markets were frozen because of a liquidity crisis. In reality, they had jammed tight because creditors feared insolvency. Central banks were dealing with the symptoms not the cause of the crisis.

Indeed, to make room on its balance sheet for liquidity injections, the Federal Reserve sold Treasuries in April 2008. As Figure 3.1 shows, the size of the central bank's balance sheet remained broadly unchanged during the time of these 'support' operations. But the level of Treasuries held by the US central bank fell sharply.[10]

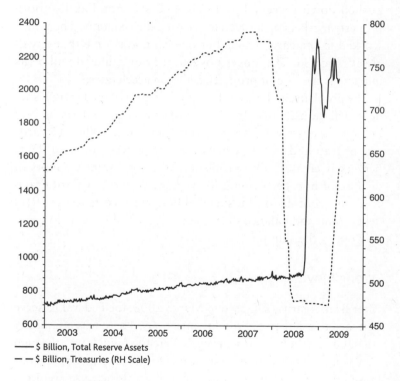

——— $ Billion, Total Reserve Assets
− − $ Billion, Treasuries (RH Scale)

Figure 3.1   US Federal Reserve Assets

Source: Federal Reserve

The policy made no sense. Selling Treasuries was the exact opposite of the policy implemented from April 1932 onwards. It was even at odds with the very limited attempts to reflate taken in 1929 and 1930. The Fed's actions following the collapse of Bear Stearns pushed borrowing costs up when they needed to fall. Without a swift cut in mortgage rates, there was no chance that house prices would stabilise. More banks would inevitably suffer the same fate as Bear Stearns.

The housing market continued to spiral down. The number of borrowers in arrears carried on rising. Over the summer of 2008, repossessions or foreclosures soared to more than three times the peak of the previous housing market crash in the early 1990s. By the end of September 2008, one in ten US homeowners with a mortgage was either in arrears or being foreclosed. That would climb to more than one in nine by the end of the year, and at least one in eight by March 2009.[11]

Following the nationalisation of Freddie Mac and Fannie Mae on 7 September 2008, the Federal Reserve shifted its monetary tactics. The giant lenders had seen their share prices slide precipitously over the summer amid heavy losses sustained from soaring repossessions.

The Federal Reserve again injected liquidity and provided emergency loans, as the financial system teetered on the brink of collapse. On this occasion, the central bank's balance sheet was allowed to expand rapidly. Some financial commentators claimed the Fed was finally engaged in quantitative easing. Indeed, the Fed's balance sheet doubled in less than two months.[12]

However, the Bank of Japan increased its balance sheet during the 1990s trying to bail out banks. That was not quantitative easing, and neither was the US action. Using a bigger balance sheet to inject liquidity did not bring down borrowing costs. It completely missed the target.

After the US Treasury Secretary Hank Paulson announced plans on 14 October 2008 to follow the UK's lead and recapitalise banks, share prices rallied. However, by the end of the month, the stock market was sliding again. At the close of trading on 24 November, Citigroup had lost nearly 90 per cent of its value from the 2006 peak.[13] The shareholder run had not yet mutated into a fatal, mass withdrawal of funds that had brought down

Bear Stearns and Lehman Brothers. Rather than wait for that inevitability, the US authorities intervened and injected $306 billion to prop up the bank.[14]

Less than 48 hours later, the Federal Reserve belatedly announced that it would try to get mortgage rates down. Later dubbed 'credit easing', the policy initially involved buying $600 billion of the debt or bonds issued by housing-related government-sponsored enterprises.[15] These included Freddie Mac and Fannie Mae, who had issued mortgage bonds to fund explosive growth in lending during the bubble. Previous liquidity injections had failed – this more direct intervention would surely do the trick policymakers hoped.

Some claimed the Fed was finally moving towards a policy of quantitative easing reminiscent of the early 1930s. In truth, it was not the same as the policy that worked in the Great Depression. The Fed was again expanding its balance sheet. And this was a more targeted attempt to drive down borrowing costs, compared with the ineffectual policies adopted since the summer of 2007. By pushing down the yields on mortgage bonds, rates would be nudged lower. It was the Fed's most direct attack on borrowing costs yet.

Mortgage Rates Start To Fall

The initial response was encouraging. Because the Federal Reserve would be buying such a large proportion of these bonds outstanding – it drove their price up and the yield down.[16] Lower yields would equate to cheaper mortgages for some.

There were three problems. The drop in mortgage rates was woefully inadequate given how far property prices had fallen. Two months after the policy had been announced, the standard 30-year mortgage rate – only available for borrowers with a 20 per cent deposit or equity in their house – was still 5.0 per cent. It had fallen just 1.8 per cent from the peak reached more than two years earlier.

During the bear market of the early 1990s – a far smaller housing crisis – the 30-year mortgage rate fell 4.0 per cent. On this occasion, the drop in property prices on the S&P/Case-Shiller index reached 6.3 per cent y/y at its worst point. By the time the Fed had unveiled its plan in November 2008 to start buying mortgage bonds, house prices on this measure were falling 19.1 per cent y/y (see Figure 3.2).[17] In contrast to the successful reflation engineered in the early 1990s, the Fed had delivered less than half the cut in borrowing costs for a housing market that was falling three times as fast. Furthermore, debt outstanding was much higher. The personal sector debt to disposable income ratio had risen from 79.2 per cent in early 1988, to 138.4 per cent 20 years later (see Figure 3.3).[18]

—— % Change year-on-year

Figure 3.2   US House Prices

Source: S&P/Case-Shiller Home Price Index, 10-City Composite

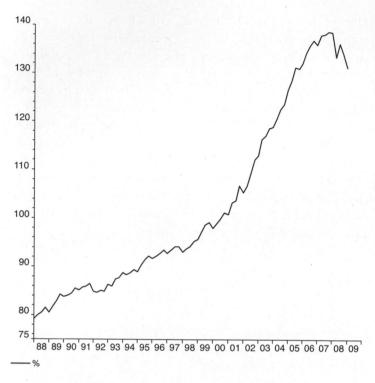

Figure 3.3   US Personal Sector Debt/Disposable Income

Source: Federal Reserve (FoF), Financial Liabilities, Households & Nonprofits and Department of Commerce, Disposable Personal Income

The 'standard' mortgage rate had not fallen anywhere near enough. But for many borrowers, the cost of borrowing was significantly higher. As house prices slid, a growing number of homeowners fell deep into negative equity. When they tried to refinance their mortgages, the cost of borrowing would rise. Credit scores also deteriorated as debtors missed repayments on their credit cards, home equity or auto loans. Rising unemployment was corroding the credit rating of borrowers. Lower credit ratings in turn pushed borrowing costs higher.

Numerous attempts by the US authorities and banks to modify loans had failed. Even at this stage, the scale of the pending housing catastrophe and the need for more aggressive action was self-evident. For all these reasons, the plan to buy mortgage bonds was inadequate.

Furthermore, corporate borrowing costs continued to rise. Bond yields for 'non-investment' grade companies rose to a punitive 22 per cent.[19] Few companies could survive at such stratospheric rates. Borrowing costs were closely correlated with job losses, unemployment was sure to leap (see Figure 3.4). Rate cuts were not working. Liquidity injections had failed too.

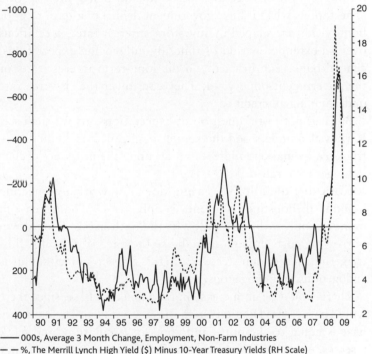

——— 000s, Average 3 Month Change, Employment, Non-Farm Industries
— — %, The Merrill Lynch High Yield ($) Minus 10-Year Treasury Yields (RH Scale)

Figure 3.4   US Job Losses and Corporate Borrowing Costs

Source: Bureau of Labor Statistics

Another False Start

On 16 December 2008, the Federal Reserve belatedly announced that it was considering the possibility of proper quantitative easing.

Following its final meeting of the year, the FOMC (Federal Open Market Committee, the body that sets monetary policy) declared it was 'evaluating the potential benefits' of Treasury purchases.[20]At long last, it seemed, the Fed was ready to embrace the policy that had finally stopped the rot in 1932.

The aim was ostensibly to reduce the 'risk-free' rate, and thus encourage other borrowing costs to fall, including corporate and mortgage rates. The very essence of this policy is the attack on interest rates. A central bank can influence interest rate expectations when it buys government debt. Long-term rates or bond yields are shaped by investors' interest rate expectations over an extended period of time. By influencing expectations, central banks can bring down the long-term interest rate, or the government bond yield. They can lower the risk-free rate underpinning all credit costs.

But it is not just a question of expectations. As we shall see, Keynes also understood the subtle significance of 'illiquidity' – triggered by market failure – in preventing the necessary decline in longer term rates.

Critically, quantitative easing does not work by injecting liquidity or boosting the money supply *per se*. The increase in money supply will only follow if the authorities bring down borrowing costs enough to stabilise the pace of defaults, thus triggering an economic recovery. In this respect, money supply is endogenous, not exogenous.

There would be an increase in the monetary base, since there would be increased liquidity in the money markets. The monetary base is equal to the notes and coins in circulation, and bank reserves. As such, it is a narrow and incomplete measure of money supply.

When a central bank buys or withdraws government debt, there would initially be more 'money in circulation', as it would pay for these bonds with a cheque written against itself. This is where the term printing money derives, even though this is not the critical point of this policy.

There was no guarantee that the increase in monetary base would lead to more lending or higher money supply growth, based on broader aggregates. The increased liquidity could simply return to the banks' accounts at the central bank. After all, the monetary base had expanded sharply in Japan during the late 1990s, without any impact on lending.[21] The increased notes and coins in circulation might not be used to create fresh loans if the borrowing rate was not driven low enough in the first place, as the Japanese authorities discovered. Lending rates are the critical test and target for this policy, not money supply.

Much of the misunderstanding over quantitative easing reflected the same confusion that bedevilled monetary policy after the money market crisis had erupted in the summer of 2007.[22] Wrongly, central banks had assumed injecting liquidity would be enough, and ignored the importance of lowering debt servicing costs. Ironically, the Bank of England was guilty of this misapprehension, even though it was the first central bank to commit to quantitative easing.

Reversing the Tide

Quantitative easing would give central banks a fighting chance of reversing the tide of corporate and household defaults, if they acted quickly. And it would work through several mechanisms.

Taking government debt out of the market and putting it on the books of a central bank, would reduce funding pressures. The sheer weight of government debt issuance was proving a major handicap to any economic recovery by late 2008 and early 2009. This was the classic crowding out problem. If institutional investors are purchasing government debt, there is much less scope for them to buy distressed assets, including corporate and mortgage bonds, thus bringing down the borrowing costs for companies and householders.

But the policy also works in other less obvious and more indirect channels. A lower risk-free rate tends to reduce investors' required rate of return on other assets. Effectively, the government bond yield is the foundation used for pricing and selling other types of debt issued by companies, banks and institutions.[23] Keynes made the point repeatedly during the 1930s.[24]

It is the impact on the risk-free rate that makes quantitative easing effective. The policy does more than free-up private sector resources to buy riskier debt. It encourages risk averse private sector funds back into the credit market. In this sense, it works as a credit multiplier, by drawing larger sums of private capital back into assets with beaten down prices.

And an important aspect of this policy is the impact on confidence from anchoring interest rates. Investors will only return to the fray in sufficient numbers when they are confident that central banks will keep rates pegged at ultra low levels. If investors suspect that central banks are not committed to such a policy, it will not succeed. Keynes was quite clear on this point:

> A monetary policy which strikes public opinion as being experimental in character or easily liable to change may fail in its objective of greatly reducing the long-term rate of interest...may tend to increase almost without limit in response to a reduction in (the rate of interest) below a certain figure. The same policy, on the other hand, may prove easily successful if it appeals to public opinion as being reasonable and practicable and in the public interest, rooted in strong conviction, and promoted by an authority unlikely to be superseded.[25]

In other words, if central banks are not committed to keeping long-term rates low – when they palpably have the very weapons to secure such an objective – investors would not be persuaded to take the extra risks in a deflationary environment. The debt trap would intensify as investors sought liquidity and safety.

Making Quantitative Easing Work

At this stage, it is tempting to wonder whether the policy would really work. The transmission mechanisms appear nebulous. But it worked in the early 1930s. And the need for such a policy can be seen from reviewing the experience of the early 1990s, and again considering the problem with the zero bound.

To recap, the 30-year mortgage rate fell by nearly 4 per cent in response to the last housing crisis between 1989 and 1993. That was possible in part because the Federal Reserve had ample scope to cut short-term interest rates, which fell from just under 10 per cent to 3 per cent. This drop of 7 per cent helped to push the Treasury bond yield down 3.5 per cent. Because it fell a long way, mortgage rates in turn dropped relative to Treasury bond yields.[26]

In other words, as the risk-free rate fell sharply, this risk premium or spread for mortgages eased too, reinforcing the decline in borrowing costs. The Fed turned a vicious circle into a virtuous cycle, and eventually stabilised the housing market.

Figure 3.5   US Fed Funds Target, 1989 to 1993

Source: Thomson Reuters Datastream

In mitigation, from 2007 onwards, the Fed could and still did cut its key lending rate by more than in the early 1990s. The fall from 5.25 per cent in the summer of 2007 to virtually zero by the

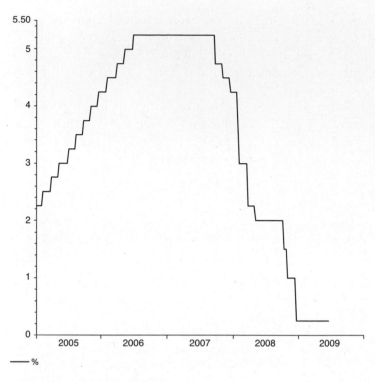

Figure 3.6   US Fed Funds Target, 2005 to 2009

Source: Thomson Reuters Datastream

end of 2008 was a relatively bigger reduction compared to that seen between 1989 and 1993. But it was delivered too slowly. Furthermore, in the absence of aggressive quantitative easing, it was much harder to effect a commensurate reduction in long-term interest rates, critical for mortgages and corporate borrowing costs. As a result, the 'real' cost of borrowing remained elevated (see Figures 3.9 and 3.10).

This was precisely the point made by Keynes during the 1930s, when he argued for *debt management policies* to drive long-term rates down. He warned that it would prove difficult to secure the same reduction in long-term rates compared to the short rate or the central bank rate. That did not matter in the early 1990s

Figure 3.7   US 10-Year Treasury Yields, 1989 to 1993

Source: Thomson Reuters Datastream

because the Fed acted swiftly. The need for quantitative easing in 2008 was amplified by the failure to get short rates down in time.

Keynes couched his argument in terms of liquidity preference. Critically, the relationship between the price and yield on a government bond is not linear. As the yield falls to ultra low levels, bond prices tend to rise ever more quickly. This is arguably one of Keynes's most important insights, so lost on policymakers today.[27]

However, investors stand to lose significant capital if the yields on bonds climb suddenly. And since these low yields might not be considered normal, it can be hard to persuade investors to hold

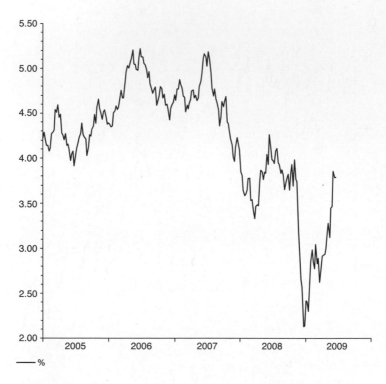

Figure 3.8   US 10-Year Treasury Yields, 2005 to 2009

Source: Thomson Reuters Datastream

these bonds without a high degree of assurance from the central bank. There was the potential for massive market failure, labelled as a liquidity trap by Keynes. It was perhaps a misnomer, since a liquidity trap did not mean a shortage of liquidity, quite the opposite. It was meant to describe the risk aversion of investors. Their desire to avoid illiquidity, with investors fretting over their inability to sell risky assets in frozen markets, was stopping rates from falling.

The argument is covered in more detail in Chapter 7 of *The Credit Crunch*. Since its publication, there has been ample evidence of the potential difficulties outlined by Keynes. Bond auctions have become much more difficult in many countries, as

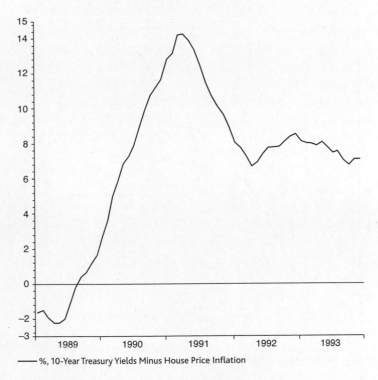

— %, 10-Year Treasury Yields Minus House Price Inflation

Figure 3.9   US 'Real' Borrowing Costs, 1989 to 1993

Source: Thomson Reuters Datastream and S&P/Case-Shiller Home Price Index,
10-City Composite

investors baulked at buying so much government debt at such
historically low yields. In the US, bond yields became hyper-
sensitive to announcements from the US Treasury detailing the
numerous auctions held to fund the huge deficit. In the UK, the
Debt Management Office was forced to enlist the help of bankers
to sell government bonds or gilts, at a cost of £14 million to the
taxpayer. Banks that had caused the credit crunch, triggering the
huge rise in the budget deficit, were now being paid to help the
government raise funds.[28]

For much of 2008, bond yields did not drop in line with short-
term interest rates. Central banks were slashing their lending

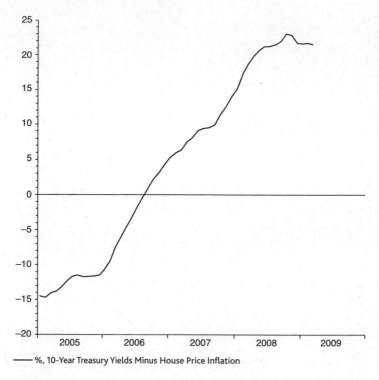

── %, 10-Year Treasury Yields Minus House Price Inflation

Figure 3.10 US 'Real' Borrowing Costs, 2005 to 2009

Source: Thomson Reuters Datastream and S&P/Case-Shiller Home Price Index, 10-City Composite

rates, but yields fell slowly. This was precisely the problem that bedevilled Japan's response to its long slump, as bond yields rose relative to the Bank of Japan's key lending rate, the Discount rate. Indeed, it was the single biggest cause of Japan's long slump.[29]

A Bond Bubble?

There were still, however, voices railing against this attack on long-term interest rates, the direct attempt to cut borrowing costs and reverse the rising tide of repossessions. There were the habitual claims that 'letting the printing press roll' would threaten a resurgence of inflation.

These fears reflected the same misguided analysis that led to monetary policy remaining too tight during the early stages of the credit crunch – notably after the collapse of Bear Stearns. Critics of quantitative easing failed to recognise that the policy was designed to keep homeowners in their houses and prevent companies from defaulting. This was hardly a precursor to hyperinflation, merely an attempt to reverse a deflation spiral.

That did not stop some commentators talking of a 'bond bubble'.[30] When the policy of quantitative easing was reversed, the cost for central banks and other investors who had bought bonds at very low yields could be calamitous. As yields rose, the price of these bonds would fall sharply.

There might indeed come a time when central banks did want to 'tighten' monetary policy. But there were other avenues through which policy could be tightened if and when the economic cycle turned. Varying capital ratios and reserve requirements for banks were potential tools at the disposal of central banks. Indeed, as we saw earlier, reserve requirements were used to devastating effect in the US during 1936 and 1937, triggering a pointless recession.[31]

Keynes had a very clear prescription. It was better to restrain lending through credit controls rather than immediately reverse the policy of low interest rates. And capital controls would be important, to allow central banks the freedom and flexibility to implement such policy weapons.[32] It was precisely the overt use of interest rates to manage the economy in a liberalised era that had precipitated boom and bust. This lack of restraint on the banks had made it impossible to control the economy through interest rates.

Charles Bean, the Bank of England's deputy governor and former chief economist, acknowledged this point when he argued that raising interest rates during the boom would have been ineffective in quelling runaway house prices: 'I have to say I think people who take the view, well, if interest rates have only been 25 or 50 basis points [0.25 per cent or 0.5 per cent] higher, none of this would have happened, are frankly rather unrealistic.' Interest rates would have needed to be 2 or 3 per cent higher to have 'significantly impacted on the build-up of credit and the asset prices, particularly house prices'. And that would have caused a recession anyway. There was clearly a need for 'a second instrument', Mr Bean admitted.[33]

In short, those who argued that driving down long-term interest rates was dangerous, simply assumed that the laissez-faire 'framework' that had caused so much strife would remain unchanged, unaltered by the cataclysmic events of the previous two years. That was unrealistic and counterproductive. The world would have to change, and in a way that would make an alternative policy regime more likely, but necessary too. In practical terms, quantitative easing could work. It would have to work if the policymakers wanted to rescue the economy within the confines of the existing system.

Whether it would actually succeed depended on timing and aggressive implementation. By leaving it so late, the impact of the policy had been diluted. Every month of delay magnified the force of deflation and the distress within the financial system.

At Last...

Bond yields did finally begin to drop during the final weeks of 2008, partly in response to 'credit easing'. But yields were also falling because of the slump in economic activity and the sudden reversal in inflation. Commodity prices were tumbling. In the US, the index for crude material prices, a good indicator of raw material costs, fell by 32.4 per cent during the three months to November. With food and oil excluded, prices were down 39.8 per cent, nearly three times the previous record decline.[34]

The global economy was spiralling into its deepest post-war recession. In the US, consumer spending plummeted with new vehicle sales dropping by a third.[35] Business surveys reported a collapse in confidence.[36]

The announcement that the Fed was going to buy mortgage bonds and was considering buying Treasuries did, more than likely, have an impact. Between 25 November and 18 December 2008, the 10-year Treasury yield fell from 3.35 per cent to 2.08

per cent. Corporate bond yields and mortgage rates started to drop too.[37]

Bernanke's Darkest Day

On 13 January 2009, Ben Bernanke travelled to London to deliver an important keynote speech on monetary policy. The markets were waiting for confirmation that 1930s-style reflation had arrived.[38]

Mortgage rates were belatedly coming down – for those borrowers not in negative equity. However, they needed to fall a long way to absorb the enormous backlog of unsold properties and stabilise house prices.[39] Corporate borrowing costs had to ease quickly too, to prevent job losses spiralling upwards, feeding into more repossessions and even bigger drops in house prices.

But the Fed chair pulled back, pouring cold water on the prospect of large scale Treasury purchases. Dismayed, bond investors sold and yields started to rise. The Federal Reserve had squandered a major opportunity to drive borrowing costs down. The drop in mortgage rates and corporate borrowing costs stalled, and the stock market resumed its long slide. The Dow Jones Industrials fell by nearly a quarter following Mr Bernanke's disavowal of quantitative easing (see Figure 3.11).[40]

The market eventually pulled out if its headlong slide. After much prevarication, Treasury Secretary Timothy Geithner unveiled on 23 March 2009 the Public-Private Investment Plan (PPIP), the latest scheme to wean banks off crippling bad debts.[41] The plan met with a rapturous response from Wall Street, with some of the biggest asset managers claiming this would finally succeed in unclogging credit markets and get banks lending again.

But the PPIP was no different from the myriad of liquidity injections that had already failed to stabilise the economy. It was based on a false premise that the collapse in the mortgage bonds had been due to a lack of liquidity.[42] Under this latest plan, banks would sell their unwanted toxic loans to asset managers, who in turn would receive a subsidy from the government. The asset managers, with government help, would be providing

Figure 3.11   US Stock Market

Source: Thomson Reuters Datastream

the missing liquidity – the oil needed to grease the wheels of capital markets.

Banks could then raise fresh capital from private sources to repair gaping holes on their balance sheets, losses created in part from selling these loans at knock-down prices. Rehabilitated banks could then start lending.

There was nothing in the plan that would stop house prices falling. Even if all the building blocks in the PPIP fell into place – and there were many risks – the absence of markedly lower borrowing costs implied house prices would continue to spiral down. The destruction of paper wealth would intensify, pulling consumer spending down and pushing unemployment up faster.

More homeowners would default. The PPIP completely missed the target.

In mitigation, the Obama administration saw the PPIP as merely one part of its policy arsenal. The Fed had come under intense pressure to do more to rescue the housing market and follow the Bank of England's lead. On 5 March 2009, the UK central bank had stolen a march on the Fed, becoming the first central bank during the credit crunch to announce quantitative easing.[43]

Put on the defensive by the Old Lady of Threadneedle Street, the Fed capitulated, announcing on 18 March 2009 that it would buy $300 billion of Treasuries. But the bulk of the Federal Reserve's balance sheet would still be devoted towards credit easing. A further $850 billion would be used to buy mortgage bonds.[44] A total of $1.75 trillion was being committed to buying bonds, but by far the larger proportion was being devoted to credit easing. This was a token shift to quantitative easing to appease critics.

The Treasury purchases were after all a mere fraction of the budget deficit likely to be incurred by the Obama administration. On official estimates, the Federal deficit was heading for $1.80 trillion.[45] Buying $300 billion of Treasuries was not going to have much impact on bond yields or borrowing costs, when the US administration was issuing six times this amount to fund its budget deficit. And so it proved. By late April, the 10-year Treasury yield had risen back above 3.0 per cent. By early June, it had soared to nearly 4.0 per cent.[46] This was nothing like the policy adopted in 1932, 1933 or 1934.

If the Federal Reserve had committed all of its ammunition to driving Treasury yields or the risk-free rate lower, it might have made some inroads into the high borrowing costs. Instead, Treasury yields were now far above the December 2008 low when the Fed had first flirted with a shift to 1930s-style reflation. They were higher than the levels of late November too, when the FOMC had unveiled its botched strategy of credit easing.

Repossessions Soar

The poverty of the Obama administration's policy during the early months was underlined by a surge in notifications from banks of their intent to repossess. More than 1 million households received foreclosure notices between March and May 2009.[47] Reprieved by multiple bail-outs and no end of liquidity injections from the Federal Reserve, banks were moving to foreclose on homeowners in record numbers, even as the same financial institutions were receiving funds from the US administration to modify mortgages.[48]

The banks had agreed to a series of moratoria on repossessions soon after President Obama took office. Administration officials had requested some breathing space as they devised plans to allow homeowners to reduce their mortgage payments. The Making Home Affordable Program was duly launched with much fanfare on 23 March 2009. It would, claimed President Obama, allow 4 to 5 million homeowners to refinance debt and remain in their homes. Overall, up to 9 million people would benefit.[49]

The headlines were compelling, but the detail showed the plan was lacking in ambition. Homeowners could, if successful, secure a reduction in interest payments on their first mortgage to 31 per cent of their *gross* income. Even a modification down to 31 per cent of *net* income would have been ungenerous. Furthermore, this reduction did not take into account second mortgages, or other debts, including credit card and auto loans.[50]

For many homeowners, the Obama plan was inadequate. Even if they did succeed in securing a cut in their mortgage payments, many were likely to default. Credit rating agency Fitch estimated that up to 75 per cent of modifications being carried out through the Making Home Affordable Program would default within six months to a year. Getting payments on the first mortgage down to the Obama target of 31 per cent was not the problem. It was all the other debts. Many of these were so high, that a large proportion of homeowners could not afford any payment on their first mortgage.[51]

The Making Home Affordable Program also needed to be far more robust to offset the deflationary impact of foreclosures triggered by the financial collapse of September and October 2008. The authoritative National Delinquency Survey, published by the Mortgage Bankers Association on 25 May 2009, underlined the timidity of the Obama response. Despite the moratoria agreed to by banks during the first quarter of 2009, the number of foreclosures initiated had soared, from 1.01 per cent of all loans in Q4 2008, to 1.34 per cent (see Figure 3.12).[52] It was an increase of a nearly a third, by far the biggest quarterly rise since records began in 1972.

Figure 3.12   US Foreclosures Started

Source: Mortgage Bankers Association, Residential Mortgage Loans, All Foreclosures Started

The cumulative number of borrowers at various stages of the foreclosure process had risen to 3.85 per cent of all homeowners, again a record (see Figure 3.13).[53] It would of course, have been higher without the moratoria.

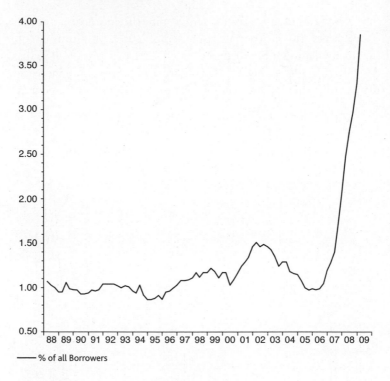

Figure 3.13   US Borrowers In Foreclosure

Source: Mortgage Bankers Association, Residential Mortgage Loans, All Foreclosure Inventory

How much higher could be gleaned from the data on delinquencies. A record 9.12 per cent of all homeowners with a mortgage were in arrears by the end of March 2009, up from 7.88 per cent at the end of 2008 (see Figure 3.14).[54] However, arrears of more than 90 days had surged from 2.75 per cent of all loans to 3.53 per cent over the comparable period.[55] In short, the lion's share of the increase in arrears came from the most critical category of '90 days or more' (see Figure 3.15).

Fannie Mae, the giant lender now owned by the US government, was quite clear about the source of this huge increase. Many borrowers had not been moved into foreclosure and were still being classified as delinquent, in an attempt to give loan modifications a chance of succeeding.[56]

% of all Borrowers

Figure 3.14   US Homeowners Delinquent

Source: Mortgage Bankers Association, Residential Mortgage Loans, All Total Delinquent

However, borrowers were also being held back from repossession because of the difficulty in processing so many delinquent borrowers. And there was a further worrying reason for the delay. Large numbers of foreclosed properties being taken to auction were being returned to banks, unsold. In May 2009, 87.9 per cent of properties taken to auction in California failed to find a bid, despite many being offered for a discount of half or more.[57]

Across the US, banks already had an estimated 700,000 empty properties sitting on their books. They hardly wanted to add to the burden.[58] Indeed, with such huge price cuts failing to attract any buyers, banks were holding back on foreclosures to minimise

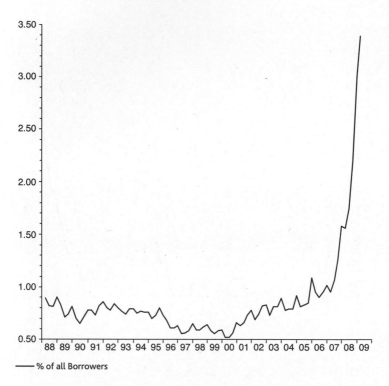

Figure 3.15   US Homeowners Delinquent, 90+ Days

Source: Mortgage Bankers Association, Residential Mortgage Loans, All 90+ Days Delinquent

their losses. If they pushed borrowers into default aggressively, they would default too.

The crisis had its roots in sub-prime and there was still no sign of that abating. By the end of March 2009, nearly one in four borrowers was in arrears (see Figure 3.16). Sub-prime arrears had risen by a quarter since the end of September 2008. But prime borrowers were beginning to suffer too. The number of delinquent prime borrowers had risen by nearly 40 per cent over the same period (see Figure 3.17).[59] The unemployment created by the collapse of Lehman Brothers was, proportionately, driving a bigger increase in prime delinquency.

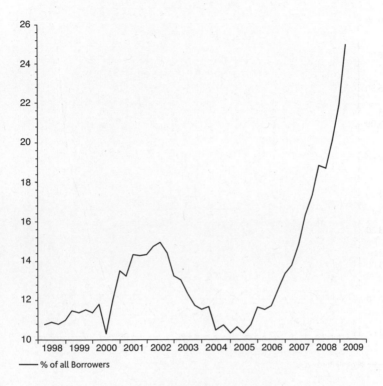

Figure 3.16   US Homeowners Delinquent, Sub-Prime

Source: Mortgage Bankers Association, Residential Mortgage Loans, Sub-Prime, Total Delinquent

In total, 12.97 per cent of homeowners with a mortgage – more than one in eight – were in arrears, or being foreclosed by the end of March 2009 (see Figure 3.18).[60] Based on the RealtyTrac data, that was set to hit one in seven by the end of June.

But the stock market continued to rally, oblivious to the realities of life for millions as they struggled to remain in their homes. A year on from the collapse of Bear Stearns, markets were trying to convince themselves that the rules of the game had not changed and capitalism had escaped, emerged unscathed from the sub-prime debacle.

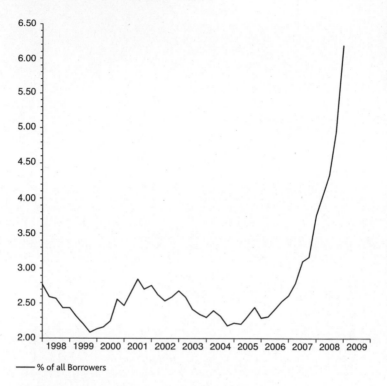

── % of all Borrowers

Figure 3.17   US Homeowners Delinquent, Prime

Source: Mortgage Bankers Association, Residential Mortgage Loans, Prime, Total Delinquent

Academics and Practitioners

The Federal Reserve chair Ben Bernanke built his academic reputation on studying the depression of the 1930s. He was also a vocal critic of Japan's inaction in the late 1990s, as the dotcom bubble imploded. To many in financial markets, it has been perplexing that an 'expert' on deflation economics could have made the same mistakes that drove the US into depression in the 1930s.

Mr Bernanke's work may be revered in academic circles. In reality, the Fed chair spent little time analysing the policies of reflation adopted by the Federal Reserve during the early 1930s.

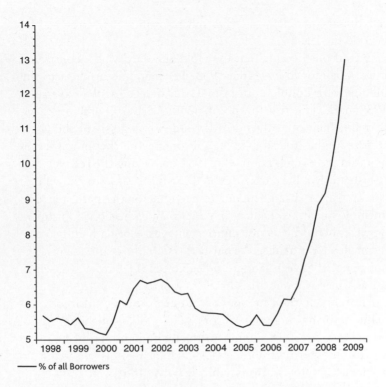

— % of all Borrowers

Figure 3.18   US Homeowners, Delinquent and In Foreclosure

Source: Mortgage Bankers Association, All Total Delinquent and All Foreclosure Inventory

His book *Essays on the Great Depression* published in 2000 contains few references to open market operations or quantitative easing.[61] His analysis of monetary policy is sketchy at best.

Mr Bernanke accepts that the contraction of money supply was the chief cause of the 1930s depression. But that 'was itself the result of a poorly managed and technically flawed international monetary system' – in other words, the Gold Standard.[62]

As we have seen, that view is too simplistic. There were policy measures that could have been taken to counteract the deflationary bias of the Gold Standard. Keynes railed routinely against the Gold Standard. But that did not stop him advocating aggressive reflationary policies – and his sphere of influence stretched far beyond the UK.

Even if one accepts that the Gold Standard was a constraint, it was abandoned in March 1933. The manufacturing sector hit the first of a double bottom in 1932. Indeed, as we have seen, 1932 marked the true low point, not the early 1993 relapse as Mr Bernanke and others claim. Any in-depth analysis of the Great Depression has to evaluate the role of open market purchases or quantitative easing, notably in 1932, in driving the recovery.

Instead, Mr Bernanke devoted far more time to the role of 'sticky wages' in an attempt to account for the persistence of unemployment. According to Mr Bernanke, the slow adjustment of wages in the face of unemployment was 'especially difficult' to reconcile or rationalise.[63] That betrays a failure to recognise the imbalances between labour and capital in the late 1920s, which caused the economic crisis in the first place.

Another chapter in Ben Bernanke's book explores 'non-manufacturing financial factors, such as banking panics and business failures'. In summary, 'the malfunctioning of financial institutions during the early 1930s' had 'real effects'. He also warned that 'Institutions which evolve and perform well in normal times may become counterproductive during periods when exogenous shocks or policy mistakes drive the economy off course.'[64] These unremarkable conclusions should have at least alerted Mr Bernanke to the risks of allowing so many mortgage lenders – and a major investment bank – to default.

And his familiarity with Japan's tortuous experience of the 1990s should have underlined the risks of acquiescing to a bubble in the first place, then moving too slowly when it inevitably burst.[65] Indeed, his analysis was sounder than much of the policy advice being offered by US economists at the time. However, criticising Japan then subsequently making the same mistakes – on a far bigger scale – shows action counts far more than words.

In the final analysis, Mr Bernanke, along with the rest of the FOMC, misjudged. But as we still argue in Chapter 5, there were ultimately deeper reasons for the policy failures.

4

GLOBALISATION AND THE RACE TO THE BOTTOM

Policy weapons were available to mitigate the slump, but they were never used in time – particularly in the US. Now, unemployment and homelessness will be an important driving force for real change, challenging the status quo seen under President Obama in his first hundred days. The stage is also set for a fraught election in the UK due by June 2010.

The 1930s offers an important insight into the importance of swift action. The collapse of so many banks left a deep scar and shattered business confidence. Unemployment eventually peaked at 25.2 per cent in the US in 1933, and then started to fall. In the UK, unemployment reached a high of 23.0 per cent in August 1932, before drifting lower.[1]

But the decline in unemployment was protracted. Governments and central banks failed to reverse the slump quickly enough. The recovery was patchy at best and stalled badly in 1937, particularly in the US.[2]

It was only the onset of the Second World War that finally galvanised the politicians into an emergency economic strategy that led to the return of full employment. A growing number of commentators today worry that capitalism is so broke that a similar outcome will follow a prolonged slump.

However, the political outcome of economic strife is not pre-ordained. The outbreak of hostilities in 1939 was not simply a reaction to failed economic policies. A key impetus to the rise of the National Socialists also came from the Versailles Treaty of 1919 and the resentment that fuelled within Germany. The invasion of the Ruhr by French troops in 1924, after Germany had failed to meet impossible reparations, stoked further widespread anger. Keynes warned in *The Economic Consequences of the Peace* that Winston Churchill's insistence on the extraction of heavy repayments from the German government would sow the seeds for the next conflict. Tragically, he was proved right.[3]

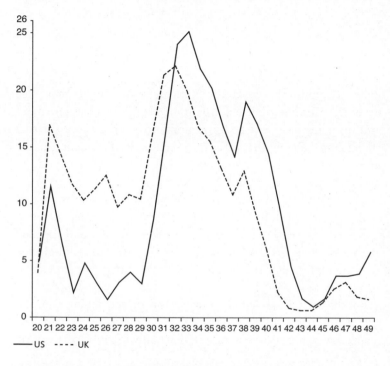

Figure 4.1   US and UK Unemployment Rate (%) 1920 to 1949

Sources: US data – Historical Statistics of the United States, Colonial Times to 1970, Part 1; UK data – Labour Market Trends

Churchill was hardly alone in seeking revenge through penal reparations. The French government pushed hard too and insisted on the terms of war reparations being honoured, right up until 1933. At that point, the collapse of the world economy led governments across the West to abandon the 1919 treaty. But the damage had been done. With the German economy suffering multiple banking failures, Hitler quickly rose to power, taking control in the same month that President Roosevelt assumed office.[4] The long march to war in Europe had begun.

Similarly, the attack on Pearl Harbor in 1941 came despite the relative success enjoyed by Japan in rebuilding its economy from the slump of the early 1930s. Deep interest rate cuts and big increases in government spending drove an economic recovery, but it was not enough to satisfy the militarists, who wanted unlimited defence expenditures.[5]

The huge rise in public spending that finally pulled the US and UK out of their long slide was military-driven too. But these increases could have taken place sooner and focused instead on non-defence areas of the economy. The Nazis succeeded in reducing the unemployment rate far better than the US and UK through a programme of sustained increases in public spending. However, much of the increased public spending was also concentrated in defence and amassing an offence capability.[6]

The US and UK governments only shifted to a more aggressive policy of reflation when the very survival of their nations was threatened. The political forces failed to secure an adequate government response for much of the 1930s until war beckoned.

If a return to full employment became possible post-1939 in response to massive government spending financed by central banks, it could have been enacted many years earlier. Instead of militarisation, it could have centred on housing – public not just private – infrastructure and an industrial renaissance.

The failure of the US and UK governments to respond until war broke out reflects the inability of the masses to force through sufficient change. The policy options used to finance the war economy were known and had been advocated by Keynes many years earlier. But not even the election of President Roosevelt, with an overwhelming mandate for change, provided the catalyst for a complete recovery that would secure full employment.

Empty Words

The comparison with 2009 is disquieting. The election of President Obama also reflects a backlash against the policies of a discredited Republican administration, rising unemployment, tumbling financial markets, sliding house prices and soaring repossessions.

Faced with a similar backdrop, President Roosevelt failed to deliver sufficient reflation.

We should not, therefore, assume that President Obama will succeed. Soon after his election victory on 4 November 2008, he pledged to create or save 2.5 million jobs. This noble aim was swiftly revised higher to a target of 3.5 million after Vice President-elect Joe Biden admitted that the economy was 'in much worse shape than we thought'.[7]

But such pledges are meaningless without a quantum shift in policy. That it required the very survival of the nation to force the US and UK governments to finally move towards full employment in 1939 and 1942 respectively underlines the political difficulty of securing the necessary response. There were policy steps that could have been taken before war broke out, but they were eschewed, in part, because the political backlash was not intense enough.

Indeed, 'centre-left' governments that argue policy is being pushed to its limits, when palpably it is not, are part of the problem, not the solution. Politicians have argued – too successfully in the past – that high unemployment was the price to be paid for breaking the wage spiral held responsible for the upsurge in inflation. It was a dubious and disingenuous argument at best. But when the scourge of price stability is deflation, there is even less justification for inaction on jobs.

Debt deflation can appear debilitating and difficult to shift because conventional policy tools fail. But there are weapons available during a time of deflation that are not options during a time of inflation. The key is securing political momentum to break with the past and operate outside of the traditional parameters.

And central to that must be a reversal of the intense squeeze on jobs and wages. The corporate drive to lower labour costs and cut jobs has accelerated during the economic downturn, as it so often does. But this time around, globalisation has coerced companies to make even bigger job cuts, notably in the US.

The incessant downward pressure on wage costs seen in the US and UK since 2000 owes much to the tendency and threat of companies to move production abroad. Anglo-Saxon countries have not been alone. Other major industrialised economies, notably Japan and Germany, have suffered from a squeeze in wages as major employers shifted jobs abroad.[8] Even before the credit crunch hit the Western consumer, wages had stagnated in many industrialised countries. In the US, the median wage was no higher in 2008 than in 2000. In the UK, it had shown only a limited rise.[9] Excessive credit growth had been made possible by the rise in so-called free trade, because that kept inflation and interest rates low. But globalisation had made the housing bubbles a necessary driver of economic growth too. The failure of governments to tackle this underlying cause of the credit crisis ensured that the fallout would be more intense. Bank bail-outs and tighter regulation have merely addressed the symptoms, not the root of the current crisis.

The squeeze on jobs has unsurprisingly stoked fears of a rise in protectionism. The long slump of the 1930s has routinely been blamed on a rise in trade barriers between countries. In truth, protectionism was on the rise long before the stock market crash of 1929.[10] Nevertheless, the increase in trade barriers as the economic downturn deepened has been widely offered as a proximate cause of the prolonged slump.

Correlation is not proof of a causal relationship. The rise in protectionism was a response to the destruction of domestic industries from intense global competition. That was fuelling the downward spiral of wages and aggravating the depression. Breaking the cycle of deflation required requisite monetary action, but it necessitated so much more. There needed to be a rebalancing of power between omnipotent capital and a weakened, enfeebled labour force.

Protectionist pressures will intensify should the current downturn persist. Already, there is a divergence opening between the Democrat-led administration in the US, ostensibly intent on rolling back the abuses of free trade, and the 'laissez-faire' Labour government in the UK. In his role as EU Commissioner and then

UK Business Secretary, Peter Mandelson has been a vocal critic of the US call for protectionism.[11]

The Prime Minister, Gordon Brown, repeatedly warned of the need not to repeat the mistakes of the 1930s, by erecting trade barriers that 'destroy jobs'.[12] And yet, the UK has seen its manufacturing base eroded at twice the pace of the US since the early 1980s.

Outsourcing, Again

As the recession began to bite, examples abounded of companies using the credit crunch as an excuse to railroad through unpopular factory closures, in the US as well as the UK.

The Credit Crunch begins with the tale of a Burberry factory in Treorchy, South Wales. It was closed in 2006 by a management trying to raise net profit margins in an attempt to boost the company's share price.[13] Production was being shifted to China, where Burberry's famed polo shirts, selling for £60 in London's upmarket Bond Street, could be made for £4.[14]

The Burberry director behind the plan to close the Treorchy factory, Evelyn Suszko, had a history of involvement in the closing of factories in Wales. Dubbed the 'axe queen', Ms Suszko had been director of operations for Laura Ashley between 1995 and 1999, when the retailer had pulled out of Wales.[15]

The relocation of the Burberry factory led to the loss of 400 jobs in the already economically marginalised Rhondda Valley. But it would boost the company's operating profits by less than 1 per cent. Every little helps when trying to impress stock market analysts, and for a short while Burberry's share price continued to rise. Then the credit crunch struck and the stock market dived. From a peak of £7.25 reached a month after the demise of the Treorchy factory, Burberry's share price tumbled to a low of £1.54 in the final weeks of 2008.[16]

Burberry's experience encapsulated the futility of all companies trying to cut labour costs, forcing credit to be the primary driver of economic growth. But it was just one of many tales that had littered nearly three decades of destruction within manufacturing.

In Merthyr Tydfil, another 300 jobs vanished when appliance manufacturer Hoover also decided it could not afford to remain in South Wales and was relocating to China and Turkey. After 60 years, the company would no longer have a production base in the UK.

Hoover's head of 'human resources' thanked the workers 'for their effort and commitment over so many years', adding, 'We wish them luck and good health in retirement, or in seeking alternative employment.'[17] The town of Merthyr had been blighted by job losses since the closure of coal mines in the area during the early 1980s. It never fully recovered, but the smattering of remaining manufacturers had provided some employment and hope, until Hoover left. It had been the town's largest private employer.

The anger at Hoover's decision to close its factory reflected a deep sense of betrayal. A generation of politicians, right and left, had failed to stand up to companies prepared to ride roughshod over workers and their communities to appease the stock market – which still ended up falling anyway. Merthyr had suffered job losses before – but this time, the rise in unemployment would be compounded by record debt and plunging house prices.

South Wales was not alone. In the East Midlands town of Peterborough, another appliance manufacturer Hotpoint shut down and moved abroad, throwing 420 out of work. These job losses were not the inevitable result of the recession. The company simply wanted to cut costs and raise margins.[18]

Time after time, layoffs were announced by companies that had not suffered from the credit crunch, but simply wanted to 'get ahead of the curve'. Demand might fall, said Stagecoach, the transport company, so it announced job cuts even as it reported record profits.[19] Pearson, owner of the Financial Times, sent an email to staff announcing 60 job losses, even as it was experiencing a boom. Rising circulation – because of the credit crunch – and repeated price increases far above inflation were driving its revenue up to record levels. But the Financial Times was looking to 'streamline' its operations.[20]

Undeterred by the local furore when it shut down its factory in South Wales and doubtless encouraged by the lack of government sanction, Burberry locked the gates to a second factory. Another 290 jobs were lost in early 2009 in the South Yorkshire town of Rotherham. Reeling from the closure of a local steelworks and the decimation of coal pits stretching back three decades, there was barely a murmur of protest from demoralised residents. 'There's nothing else round here. We're devastated', responded one employee on hearing news of the factory's demise.[21]

Burberry had shut two of its three UK factories in less than three years. Three months after the axe fell on Rotherham, the company's chief financial officer unveiled record revenues, up 21 per cent in 2008 over the previous year, boosted by wealthy Chinese visitors to London.[22] Its share price had recovered from the carnage inflicted by the collapse of Lehman Brothers. But it was still languishing at less than half its 2007 peak reached just after the closure of its Treorchy factory.

It was not just manufacturing jobs that were being lost to cheaper locations. Telephone company T-Mobile announced in early April 2009 that it was trying to save cash by shifting 500 low-paying call centre jobs to the Philippines.[23]

When the IT outsourcing specialist Logica announced a 17 per cent rise in revenues, the company's chief executive lauded a 50 per cent jump in the order pipeline since August 2008. Customers were considering 'shifting business to Logica's cheaper offshore locations such as India and Morocco'.[24]

The credit crunch might have ostensibly forced a shift in the political landscape, with a sudden penchant for state intervention in banks. But in many other critical areas, the full blast of the pro-market policies unleashed by the arrival of Reaganomics and Thatcherism in the early 1980s and late 1970s remained unrelenting.

Given the Labour Party's enthusiastic embrace of the Thatcherite doctrine, it was unsurprising that the incumbent government should eventually see its vote collapse in the European elections held in June 2009. It might have been the cradle of the Labour Party, but in Wales the Labour vote tumbled further than anywhere else in the country. Yorkshire was another stronghold for the Labour Party. Here, the collapse of the Labour vote opened the door to the far right British National Party, which secured its first ever parliamentary seat. The systematic destruction of the manufacturing base and the realisation that workers had been abandoned to their fate by market forces provided fertile breeding ground for extremists.[25]

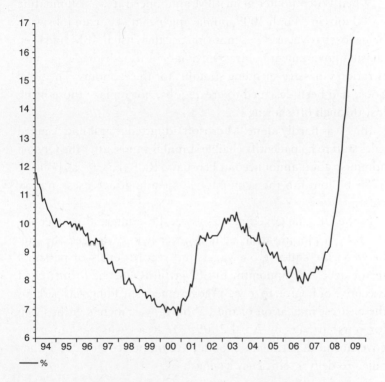

Figure 4.2   US Unemployment Rate, U6, 1994 to 2009

Source: Bureau of Labor Statistics

President Obama had pledged he would do more to protect domestic industry and jobs. But after he took power, the pace of job losses accelerated (see Figure 4.2). The Obama administration was going to try to spend its way out of recession with a huge fiscal stimulus. There was no radical agenda to intervene directly and save jobs. There was no blueprint to nationalise companies in trouble and unable to refinance onerous debt burdens. There was no direct attempt to redirect the massive excess capacity that emerged in industry towards green technology. There were no attempts to stop companies using cheaper labour abroad to cut costs, shedding jobs at home.

When US computer giant IBM announced it was eliminating 5,000 jobs in March 2009, public anger that yet again jobs were being lost to overseas was more intense than usual. IBM had been chasing government contracts available through the US administration's massive spending stimulus for the economy. The fiscal boost had been designed to create jobs, not replace those being lost through off-shoring.[26]

IBM was hardly alone. Microsoft admitted that it had 'trained sales staff to help identify eligible stimulus funds' after the Obama administration announced in February 2009 that it was pouring $787 billion into the economy via spending increases and tax cuts.[27]

In the UK, the government showed little interest in reversing the tide of globalisation. It had never acknowledged the link between the squeeze on wages and record levels of personal sector debt. The appointment of Martin Read, the former chief executive of Logica, to 'review' government spending was perhaps the clearest indication of the Labour government's enthusiasm for outsourcing. By April 2009, Mr Read was warning that government departments should have money confiscated if they failed to deliver 'efficiency savings'.[28]

Race to the Bottom

Not even the collapse of emerging markets and their exchange rates could shake the UK government's determination to drive down trade barriers, opening up more sectors of the economy to a competitive battle workers could not win. Sterling may have slumped against the dollar, the euro and the yen. But against many of the more important emerging market countries – where jobs were likely to be relocated – sterling had risen.

This had been the logical outcome of the credit bubbles seen across wide swathes of emerging market or 'developing' countries. They may have initially been the recipients of new jobs as Western companies moved production abroad. However, the wages offered to workers in many emerging market countries were not high enough to drive economic growth. That had come from excessive expansion of credit, sparked in part by Western capital inflows and by the takeover of domestic banks. Now that the capital flows had vanished, exchange rates had in many cases plummeted.

The one 'exception' was China. For the West, imports of low cost goods from China, including textiles and toys, were becoming more expensive. However, that was being offset by a relentless expansion in imports of high value goods. China had continued to industrialise at a frenetic pace. Textiles had been the biggest source of China's trade surplus, but in 2008, that was overtaken by machinery and electronic equipment (see Figure 4.3).[29]

China was 'moving up the value curve', encroaching on a wider range of industries and threatening a further decline in the remnants of manufacturing in the West. But the impetus was again Western companies relocating, not indigenous Chinese manufacturers. For the West, it still made sense to outsource. Wage rates might have been rising, but labour costs were still far lower than at home.

Even when the rise in Chinese wages during the boom had eaten into the profit margins of Western companies, there were plenty of other countries where production could be relocated. Vietnam, for example, offered much lower wages, and was providing an increasing share of the West's textiles.[30]

And once the boom came to an end, the rise in Chinese wages suddenly stalled. As Chinese exports plunged, unemployment soared.[31] By the end of 2008, 20 million migrant workers had been laid off from export factories, as a senior government official warned that the total 'will eventually reach 50 million'.[32] China was suddenly becoming competitive again. The race to the bottom was back on.

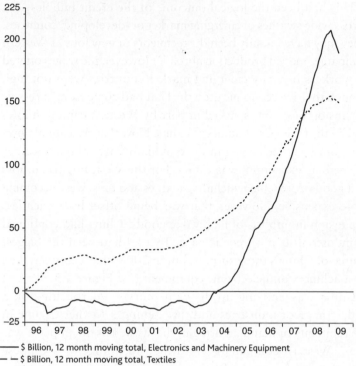

Figure 4.3   China Trade Balance

Source: General Administration of Customs

Wages in the Zero Bound

In truth, the deflationary impact from globalisation had never gone away. As the credit crunch intensified and stock markets slumped, many stores and shops were locked in a fierce, competitive battle to preserve market share.

This would not have been possible without the determination of retailers, wholesalers and suppliers to continue driving costs down in the first place, playing one emerging market off against another. After all, if they could arbitrage between wage costs in the West and emerging market economies, it was perfectly logical that the same law of the jungle would apply across emerging markets.

Indeed, if firms in the West did not seek out the lowest possible wage costs, they would lose market share to their competitors.

In systematically tearing down trade barriers without sufficient regard for the impact on workers, politicians allowed and obliged companies to drive Western economies towards a debt trap. And as the collapse in house prices hit consumer demand and ate into company profits, business leaders reacted with vengeance, slashing labour costs.

The attempts of companies to maintain profit margins seemed rational from their perspective. But it was hugely damaging. Lower wages would merely aggravate the downturn in the economy, depressing consumer spending even more.

And that would be even more of a problem when an economy was close to the 'zero bound'. Recent recessions have typically been characterised by big cuts in labour costs, but so long as there was room for monetary policy to absorb the deflationary impact on demand, the economy would eventually recover. However, if inflation was very low *a priori* and, therefore, the scope to use monetary policy limited, wage cuts could drive the economy into a debt trap, where conventional policy weapons failed.

This was hardly a new argument. This was a key difference between Keynes and the classical economists during the 1920s and 1930s. The latter argued that allowing wages to fall during a time of high unemployment was the correct policy prescription. If workers were unable to find work at the prevailing wage rate, this must indicate that labour costs were too high. Labour was treated like any other commodity, and if there was excess supply (that is, unemployment), workers had to accept a lower income if full employment was to be restored.

Keynes exposed the fallacy by showing that lower wage rates would lead to lower, not higher, rates of employment. He argued that cutting wages would depress consumer spending and reduce the demand for labour. The classical economists countered by declaring that other equilibrating forces would come into play that would restore full employment, even as wage rates fell. Lower wage rates might lead to a fall in inflation and a reduction in

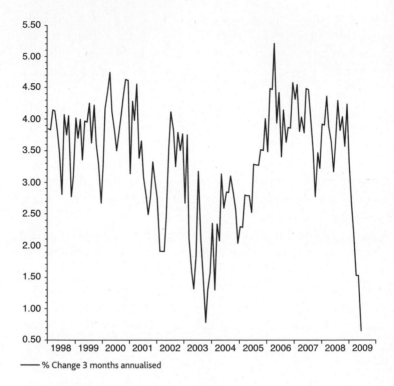

Figure 4.4   US Average Hourly Earnings

Source: Bureau of Labor Statistics

interest rates. This would help stimulate a recovery – via faster credit growth – and eventually bring unemployment down.

Essentially, that is what happened during the early 1990s, notably in the US, when the economic downturn was accompanied by significant job shedding as companies sought to rebuild profit margins. 'Downsizing' entered into the lexicon of ugly euphemisms. However, at the start of the downturn in the summer of 1989, inflation was comparatively high and there was significant potential for the Federal Reserve – and other central banks – to bring down interest rates and guide bond yields lower.[33]

When inflation is much lower *a priori*, the risks of coming up against the zero bound are greater. It is harder to get the real

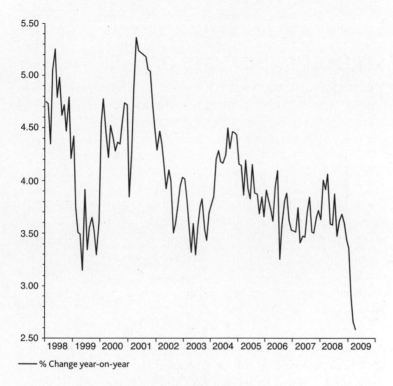

— % Change year-on-year

Figure 4.5   UK Average Earnings, Excluding Bonuses

Source: Office for National Statistics

cost of borrowing down. When inflation is low at the top of
the economic boom – as in 2008 – there is a chance that it will
soon approach negative territory, making it impossible to secure
a reduction in real borrowing costs. The problem is compounded
by the extreme levels of debt incurred during the boom. Low
inflation and record debt is a toxic combination, as the West is
now discovering.

5

STRUCTURAL CAUSES OF THE RECESSION

The first four chapters discussed the policy mistakes that brought the world economy to the brink of depression. Serious errors were made by governments and central banks in tackling the credit crisis. If they had not been mesmerised by a non-existent inflation threat, had acted sooner and taken a more radical approach, a significant part of the damage inflicted by the collapse of the credit bubble might have been averted.

However, we can only say might. We can hardly be certain. And the very fact that so many mistakes were made might not have been an accident, but symptomatic of a failed 'system'. If the economic model was so vulnerable, so prone to individual errors of judgement, might that not indicate a fundamental flaw with capitalism itself? Did the economy become so complex, so utterly impossible to manage that policymakers were doomed to fail? Were the debt levels so high, that getting the timing right with respect to rate cuts and quantitative easing was simply too much to expect? Or were policymakers doomed to failure because they were blinded by their ideology?

Questions like these are prompting a deeper discussion of Marx's theory of crisis.[1] In *The Credit Crunch*, the critique of globalisation focused on the relentless drive by companies to boost profits. The ability of corporations to roam the globe cutting labour costs in the name of free trade lay at the heart of the credit crisis that gripped the world economy in 2008. Credit was needed to fill the gap left by stagnant wages and a three-decades-long assault on organised labour.

This argument fits into a Marxist framework. Indeed, the 'law of the tendency of the rate of profit to fall' was regarded by Marx as 'the most important law from the historical standpoint'.[2] It was essential to understanding why capitalism was prone to crisis.

In essence, capitalism is based around a system of 'accumulation'. The job of capitalists is to boost profits to their limit. There can be no middle way. If a company does not exploit every potential opportunity to maximise profits, it will not survive. It will be undermined by competitors and eventually driven out of business or subsumed by a rival. Every company is forced by the law of the jungle to accumulate capital, to ensure it is not swallowed by a competitor.

— %

Figure 5.1   US Wages and Salaries/GDP

Source: Bureau of Labor Statistics, Bureau of Economic Analysis

This can, however, lead to overaccumulation. For Marx, accumulation was specifically pumping profits back into a firm, principally to purchase new or expanded plant and equipment. On an individual level, companies need to accumulate faster than their rivals to survive. But in aggregate, their combined actions can lead to excess capital in the form of plant and machinery. This ultimately leads to intense price competition, exerting downward pressure on profits in relation to investment.

This tendency for the profit rate to fall can alternatively be seen through the prism of labour costs. Companies are engaged in a competitive struggle, but the compression of wages will undermine the ability of consumers to buy and absorb the goods and services being produced. The contradictions with capitalism will eventually be exposed when consumers can no longer buy all the goods being produced.

But limited consumption and overproduction were the consequence of overaccumulation. For Marx, it was wrong to see the crisis in capitalism as merely the result of stagnation in wages (see Figure 5.1). This was a symptom of the driving force behind capitalist crises.[3]

Fiction and Capital

And Marx stressed that it was not just overaccumulation that lay behind the instability of capitalism. The growth of *fictitious* capital also sewed the seeds for crises. Capitalists would eventually struggle to put their capital to effective use. More and more of their excess funds would be driven into fictitious or speculative capital. The growth of private equity firms, mergers and acquisitions, hedge funds, complex instruments including derivatives and commercial property loans were all symptomatic of excess capital chasing a dwindling pool of real opportunities.

Indeed, 'the search for yield' was a common refrain during the final years of the credit boom. Central bankers repeatedly referred to the collapse of credit spreads and risk premiums as a manifestation of excess savings chasing lower and lower returns in financial markets. As money poured into financial markets from capital rich savers across the world, the rate of interest on many very high-risk bonds with low credit ratings collapsed to unprecedented levels.[4]

Ironically, this phenomenon was viewed as a reflection of an increasingly stable world economy.[5] Savers were content to accept a lower rate of return because the risks of investing had fallen. There were all sorts of reasons for this, but chief of all was a growing sense that independent central banks had tamed the economic cycle. Free from the clutches of political control, they were able to act quickly whenever inflation became a mild threat. There would be no return to boom and bust.

As we can now see with some clarity, these low rates of return were instead symptomatic of the underlying malaise identified by Marx. Furthermore, it was the concentration of excess funds in fictitious capital that would provide the trigger for a collapse of the credit cycle, taking the economy into recession.

The crisis would initially appear to be nothing more than a localised problem with 'money and credit'. Central bankers and similarly myopic commentators would repeatedly claim that the 'economic fundamentals are sound' stressing that any liquidity difficulties were a short-term problem. But Marx warned that 'Business is always thoroughly sound and the campaign in full swing, until suddenly the debacle takes place.'[6]

The liquidity crunch was usually a symptom of deeper, real difficulties, a chronic imbalance between capital and labour. And capital was frequently the driver and cause of the systemic breakdown.

The failure to acknowledge this fundamental point has been the source of the policy mistakes throughout today's credit crunch. The inability of central banks and governments to understand the role of capital in driving the long boom ensured their response function was severely impaired. Indeed, it is precisely because the crisis materialises in the finance system first that policymakers misread its dynamics, falling repeatedly 'behind the curve' as argued in the first four chapters of this book. They are treating the symptoms – liquidity problems – rather than the underlying causes – a surfeit of capital, fictitious and real. As a result, they fail to recognise the importance of preventing defaults, thus allowing debt deflation to take root.

When the crisis breaks, a traumatic devaluation of speculative capital quickly ensues. That in turn leads to a reduction in the availability of credit, which feeds into a collapse of demand. The overproduction then becomes apparent. The destruction of asset values destroys fictitious capital, but it also creates redundant capital in the real economy, as firms find they have spare capacity. This quickly becomes idle and much of this is written down in value too.

This climactic phase determines the nature of any upswing. An intense write-down of excess capital lays the foundations for a recovery. The process of accumulation begins anew. But the depth of the destruction during the economic downturn will determine the length and intensity of the upswing.

According to Marxists, the Second World War was followed by a long boom lasting until the early 1970s precisely because so much capital was written off or destroyed. As a result, profit rates were high during the early years of rebuilding. The contradictions of capitalism and the tendency of profit rates to fall were mitigated by war.

Countervailing Forces

War was one of a number of countervailing forces that could delay or obstruct the tendency of the profit rate to fall. Since a crisis is caused by too much capital chasing too few returns, any exogenous factor that either raises profit margins or prevents them falling, will slow down the inevitable march towards the crisis.

Marx identified a number of other countervailing forces. These included an *extension of credit*. The cut in US interest rates to a low of 1.0 per cent in 2003 to drive the housing boom was a classic example of loose monetary conditions reigniting a boom.

A reduction of 'turnover and circulation time' through faster production and sales systems, or better inventory controls is another countervailing force. This would reduce the required capacity and working capital, and so raise profit margins. The steady decline in the inventory to sales ratio for US companies – prior to the credit crisis – shows how technology has reduced the required working capital (see Figure 5.2).[7]

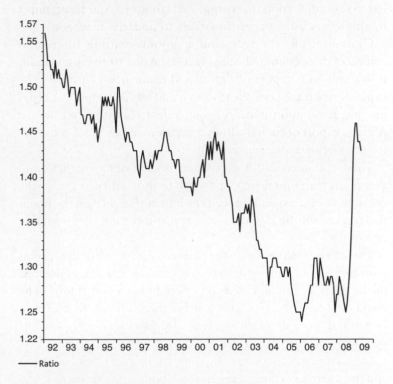

Figure 5.2   US Business Inventories to Sales Ratio

Source: Department of Commerce

Another countervailing force is the use of cheaper labour. The introduction of a minimum wage in the UK and its extension in the US under President Clinton should ordinarily have reduced the opportunities for employers to boost margins. But the commitment to a minimum wage was weak and easily circumvented, in part by the effects of outsourcing.[8]

And the surge in migration over recent years has clearly shifted the balance in favour of employers. Governments welcomed migration because, they claimed, it filled a gap in skill shortages.

In reality, it sustained the economic boom by preserving corporate margins. Politicians were never interested in protecting workers – domestic *and* migrant – from the potential impact on wages. It was left to sporadic action from organised labour to counter attempts by employers using migrant workers to undermine wages.[9]

Globalisation is a very similar countervailing force, and embraces three commonly cited factors. Aside from looser credit, it overlaps with *export of capital* and *expansion of trade*.[10] The expansion of trade between advanced and less developed countries provides new opportunities for companies to boost profit margins. And the export of capital allows companies in advanced countries to seek out cheaper production locations.

These countervailing forces wane as the boom lengthens and eventually turn into their 'opposites'. In short, they can delay the crisis, but not prevent it. Indeed the longer they sustain the boom the greater will be the force of a reversal during the inevitable downturn.

This can be seen on a number of levels. The depth of the current crisis that engulfed emerging market economies in 2008, underlined the huge risks with an extension of credit on a global level. The credit bubbles, the extreme trade imbalances, combined with even larger and more destabilising capital flows dwarf any previous meltdown in emerging market economies in modern times.

For advanced economies, the negative impact of globalisation and the disembowelling of organised labour since the early 1980s can be seen through the necessity of extreme credit growth to sustain demand in the face of a stagnant wage. To the extent that borrowing and debt were pushed to historic extremes, globalisation is indeed a countervailing force that has turned into an opposite and vicious one too.

But the role of globalisation in driving the boom lulled not only policymakers and (most) politicians into believing the world economy had entered a new era of enduring prosperity, reduced volatility, low risk premia and sky-rocketing returns.

With one or two notable exceptions, it was a view shared by most of the mainstream press.[11] Some commentators conceded that globalisation might have created worrying imbalances. But few could see the inherent inconsistencies in the ruthless manner capitalism had embraced and ultimately abused 'free trade'. Even those who did worry about trade deficits failed to draw the connection with capitalism's drive to boost margins through the export of capital.[12]

The huge returns made from investing overseas during the housing boom underlined the point. The use of cheaper production bases abroad did boost profits. But there was a dichotomy between domestic and overseas profits. That Western companies were using cheaper foreign labour to sustain high profits was not a signal that the upswing would prove more durable. It was a warning that capitalism was in crisis.

The breakdown of the profit numbers in the US underlines the point. Profits rose strongly after the dotcom recession. They did not quite reach the dizzying heights of 1950 during the long post-war boom, but they were not far short. But much of this was due to rising profits from overseas. Domestic non-financial profits rose slowly during the boom. This point is discussed in more detail from page 130 onwards.[13]

This dichotomy was strong evidence of the role played by globalisation in compressing wages at home, and thus necessitating a rise in personal debt to extreme levels. However, to reiterate, it was not underconsumption, but the drive for accumulation that has been the key dynamic behind today's economic crisis.

In essence, policymakers failed to understand the role of globalisation in causing today's credit crunch because they were deceived by the true source of their profit. Even as the crisis intensified and central banks followed mistake with mistake, mainstream politicians leapt to the defence of globalisation, claiming that without free trade, the downturn would be more intense.

But it is precisely because business leaders and their supporters in government cannot see how their profit has been earned that policymakers are prone to errors. There is a limit to the profit that can be derived from labour, but not from fictitious capital – even if rising asset prices are ultimately a zero sum game, and do not create real value.[14] As the latter soars, the capitalists are deluded into believing they have been clever, that economic management is more accomplished and lessons from the previous cycles have been learnt. Rarely is this the case.

The aversion to inflation inevitably reflects a determination of politicians and policymakers to maintain the dominance of capital over labour. Low inflation creates a self-fulfilling, virtuous circle for capitalists. It disempowers trade unions and allows interest rates to remain low. That in turn makes it easier for consumers to borrow and easier for firms to expand, accentuating the accumulation of capital. Consumers are buying goods on credit rather than through wage gains. Conversely, higher inflation creates the conditions for unions to rally and mobilise workers, leading potentially to an erosion of profits.

The China Rush

Marxist economists warned that the overaccumulation of capital would eventually 'stoke' inflation. Typically, it was claimed that 'the vast expansion of production and capital accumulation in China' had created a 'wild rush for the essential resources'.

Commodity prices did indeed soar during the stages of the economic upswing, reaching their peak in the spring of 2008. It seemed that there were different constraints affecting central banks in 2007 compared with 2001. Central banks would no longer be able to 'buy their way out of a crisis' through rate cuts.

But the deflationary impact of China as a source of cheap labour did not dwindle even as wages there rose, because it was also subsumed by an overaccumulation of capital. China was overinvesting and that would soon turn to overproduction across a vast range of consumer goods.[15]

This was compounded by a lack of protection and rights for Chinese workers, and aggravated by an unwillingness of the Chinese authorities to allow the renminbi to appreciate. Once the overcapacity became obvious, they were no longer interested in letting the renminbi rise to rebalance the world economy. Inflation was not their primary concern anymore. It was excess capacity and not enough jobs.[16]

It has already been argued in Chapters 1 and 3 that central banks were far less constrained than they – and many others – were willing to acknowledge. The rise in inflation pressures during the final months of the boom was limited given the scale of the rise in raw material costs. Throughout 2008 it was not hard to see that the property bubble had burst in many Western countries, and that fears of inflation would soon be replaced by talk of deflation.

The threat of inflation was non-existent precisely because the accumulation of capital was so acute during the upswing. And wages were failing to keep up with inflation. It is perhaps ironic: in the usual Marxist framework, the decline in real wages during 2008 gave central banks the opportunity to provide the monetary offset that would have cushioned the destruction and devaluation of capital.

But they misread the significance of this divergence between rising inflation and static wages. What could have been a classic countervailing force was nullified by the inability of policymakers to see the flaws within the economic model they had created.

Globalisation was a classic countervailing force, but it subsequently turned from being virtuous to vicious. It led to a stunning collapse in production and output, and the sudden emergence of enormous excess capacity. And it triggered a wave of job cuts, as companies reacted with a vengeance to the inevitable slump in profits by exporting more capital and squeezing labour costs.

Exporters Hit

The evidence is perhaps most striking among the economies heavily geared towards international trade. Japan was without question one of the biggest losers with a slump that surpassed the pessimists' worst fears. By February 2009, exports had nearly halved from their peak a year earlier (see Figure 5.3).[17] In the space of four months, manufacturing output plummeted 30.6 per cent (see Figure 5.4).[18] The decline was *quicker* than the reversal seen in the US over any comparable period during the Great Depression.

———— Yen Billion, Exports of Goods, Customs Basis

Figure 5.3   Japan Exports

Source: Ministry of Finance, Japan

The biggest contraction in any one year came in 1932, when production fell 21.0 per cent.[19]

The reversal in Japan's real GDP has not been as severe as the US's in the first year of the Great Depression. US real GDP fell 10 per cent in 1930.[20] Nevertheless, by the first quarter of 2009, Japan's GDP was already down 8.4 per cent (see Figure 5.5).[21] Japan has not been alone. Taiwan, Thailand, South Korea, Singapore and Malaysia have all seen precipitous declines in output.[22]

Other big exporters to suffer include Germany. Manufacturing production fell 24.1 per cent in the year to April 2009, comparable to the decline seen in the US in 1930.[23] New orders had fallen

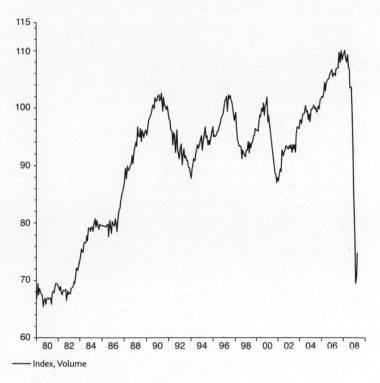

———— Index, Volume

Figure 5.4   Japan Industrial Production

Source: Ministry of Economy, Trade and Industry

35.9 per cent from their 2008 peak, led by an even bigger drop in foreign demand, of 40.7 per cent (see Figure 5.6).[24]

Sweden, with a similar exposure to world trade, was hit hard too. By January 2009, new orders for Swedish manufacturers had slumped 35.8 per cent from their January 2008 high. In Finland, they had tumbled 53.7 per cent.[25] Across Euroland, orders dropped by 34.0 per cent from their April 2008 peak, and were showing no sign of levelling out.[26] And output fell even more sharply than in either the US or UK (see Figures 5.7, 5.8 and 5.9).[27]

That was surely proof of the inherent instability within the globalised economy. Even countries that had held on to more of

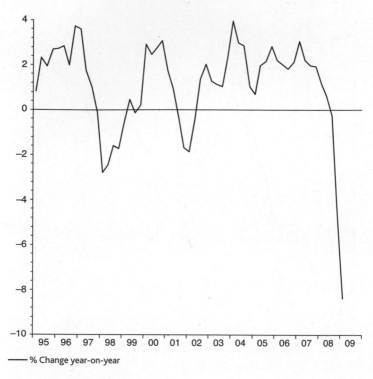

Figure 5.5   Japan Real GDP

Source: Cabinet Office (Japan)

their manufacturing were still hit hard, because they had relied upon the expansion of debt elsewhere to absorb their overproduction.

And the excess capacity that arose from collapsing output was huge. By February 2009, Japanese companies were using 43.1 per cent less capacity than a year earlier (see Figure 5.10).[28] In the US, manufacturers were operating at just 65.7 per cent of capacity by April 2009.[29] In the UK, 76 per cent of companies surveyed by the CBI admitted they had spare capacity, despite a 'beggar-thy-neighbour' devaluation of sterling in 2008.[30]

Falling output and such huge excess capacity destroyed profit margins, even as raw material costs fell. In Japan, the decline

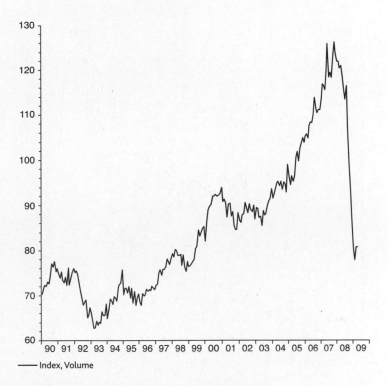

——— Index, Volume

Figure 5.6   Germany Manufacturing New Orders

Source: Deutsche Bundesbank

was seismic. Profits fell by more than two-thirds.[31] Within manufacturing, profits disappeared altogether, as industry recorded a loss for the first time on record (see Figure 5.11).[32]

In the Anglo Saxon economies, the impact on profits was mitigated by deeper cuts in labour costs. Nevertheless, corporate cash flow in the US fell by nearly a quarter following the demise of Lehman Brothers, before a surge in unemployment led to some improvement in the early months of 2009.[33]

Across the West, the decline in profits was initially driven by the rise in raw material costs, as commodity prices soared in the early months of 2008. But the biggest drop came after the credit crunch hit consumer demand. Falling demand, when firms had

Figure 5.7   Euroland Industrial Production

Source: Eurostat

already been struggling to use their available capacity, caused profits to implode.

Overinvesting

Capacity utilisation had never been that high at the top of the housing bubble. In the US, it peaked at just 79.6 per cent in manufacturing. That was lower than the top of the dotcom boom, which in turn was lower than the previous cyclical peaks. It was also significantly lower than the average of 81.0 per cent stretching back to 1950 (see Figure 5.12).[34] Companies had been struggling to sustain maximum output since the early 1970s, with

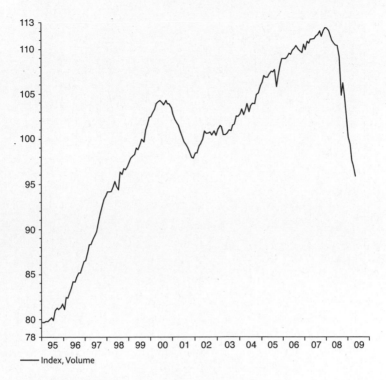

Figure 5.8 US Industrial Production

Source: Federal Reserve

progressively lower peaks at the top of each economic cycle. This was clearly manifestation of an overaccumulation in capital.

Not surprisingly, one of the most heavily impacted industries was capital goods. With so much excess capacity, there was little need to expand existing facilities. That is why Japan and Germany, both major exporters of capital goods, were hit so hard by the credit crisis of 2008. In Germany, foreign demand for capital goods tumbled by nearly half.[35] In Japan, foreign demand for machinery fell by nearly three-quarters in the year to February 2009 (Figure 5.13).[36]

Ordinarily, a collapse of investment should eventually restore the conditions for profitable accumulation. Once enough capital has been written down a recovery may ensue.

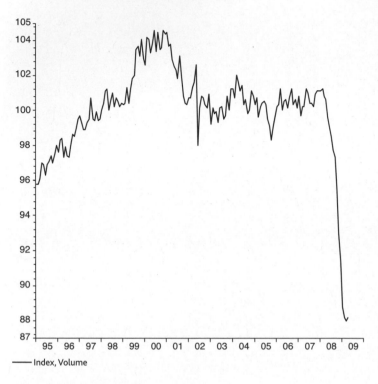

Figure 5.9   UK Industrial Production

Source: Office for National Statistics

Thus, as we have already seen, Marxist economists argue there is a clear connection between the long period of growth between 1948 and 1973, before the oil crisis struck, and the unprecedented destruction of capital, machinery, infrastructure and buildings during the Second World War. A sharp reduction in the capital stock makes new investment profitable again. The destruction of so much capital between 1939 and 1945 did restore profitability of investment, underpinning the boom. As we shall see, profit rates were very high during the post-war years.

The dynamics of a recovery seem reasonable. In theory, companies will take advantage of low wages and cheap, widely available credit. Surplus labour drawn from the masses of

— Index, Volume

Figure 5.10   Japan Capacity Utilisation

Source: Cabinet Office (Japan)

unemployed can be hired cheaply. Inventories accumulated in the crisis are sold off, production resumes and prices can once again start to rise, pushing profits higher. Investments financed by loan capital can expand again. Credit can then once again become an important driver of the economic cycle.[37]

However, as we shall see, a recovery is far from automatic. Indeed, the role of the state in driving the post-war boom is often understated. In his excellent recent book, *Zombie Capitalism*, economist Chris Harman rightly draws attention to the arms race and the 'unprecedented level of peacetime arms spending' as a critical factor in sustaining the long period of economic growth between 1948 and the early 1970s.[38]

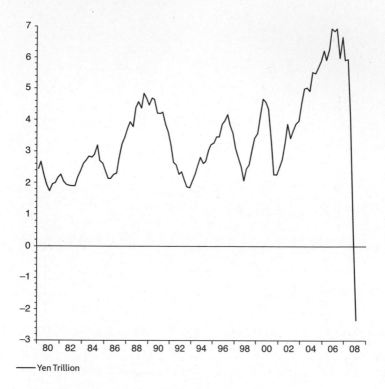

Figure 5.11   Japan Manufacturing Current Profits

Source: Ministry of Finance, Japan

Nevertheless from a Keynes perspective, we can see there are huge risks today too. The critical issue of how protracted the downturn will be necessitates a close examination of financial markets and their interaction with monetary policy. Only then can we begin to answer the question of what shape *any* recovery may take, and the considerable risks that lie ahead.

Profit Rates and the Crisis

The precise trajectory of profits has been the subject of considerable debate among economists in recent years. Data published by the Bureau of Economic Analysis in the US strongly supports the

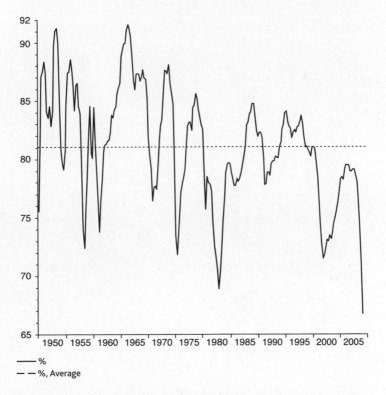

—— %
– – %, Average

Figure 5.12   US Manufacturing Capacity Utilisation

Source: Federal Reserve

argument by those who claim the economic crisis of 2008 was attributable to a declining profit rate.

Superficially, it would appear that US companies have seen a secular improvement in their profits during recent years. Looking at total profits in relation to the economy, it is hard to see why there was such a collapse into deep recession in 2008.

The ratio of profits to GDP fell sharply during the dotcom recession, dropping to 7.0 per cent in the third quarter of 2001 (see Figure 5.14). But aggressive central bank reflation, the rapid rise in house prices and a determination to keep a lid on labour costs, partly through outsourcing, saw the profits to GDP ratio climb steadily. It reached a high of 12.9 per cent in the third

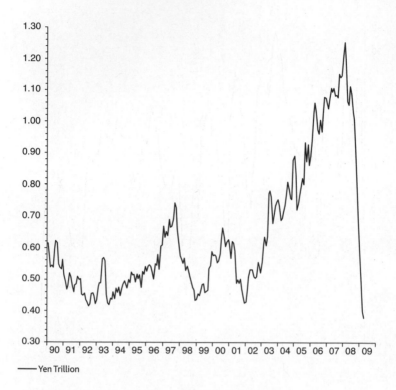

Figure 5.13   Japan Foreign Machinery Orders

Source: Cabinet Office (Japan)

quarter of 2006. This was not far short of the post-war high, when the profits to GDP ratio hit 13.3 per cent in the fourth quarter of 1950 (see Figure 5.14).[39]

Since 2006, the collapse of house prices has precipitated a swift drop in the profits to GDP ratio. It fell to 8.9 per cent by the fourth quarter of 2008, before rebounding to 9.3 per cent in Q1 2009. But there is nothing in any of this to connect profits or the over-accumulation of capital to the current credit crisis. Profits appear not to have been under pressure during the upswing. And even in the downturn, they remain above their historic low reached in the fourth quarter of 1982, when the profits to GDP ratio dropped to 6.3 per cent.

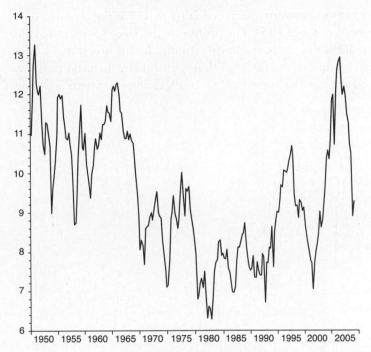

——— %, US Corporate Profits With Inventory Valuation Adjustment and Capital Consumption Adjustment/Nominal GDP

Figure 5.14   US Corporate Profits/GDP

Source: Bureau of Economic Analysis

The banking system may be in turmoil, but there is no crisis of capitalism it would appear. Regulation may need to be strengthened and lessons have to be learnt. However, the underlying economy remains sound many still claim.

But the argument by Marx was couched in terms of profit rates. There was no argument that prior to a crisis, aggregate profits might be historically high. In relation to investment outlays or capital, it was a different matter. The inner contradictions within capitalism centred on the difficulty companies faced in trying to sustain profits in relation to a growing mass of capital.

Nevertheless, the ratio of profits to investment spending did rise during the housing boom, climbing from a cyclical low of 61.2

per cent in the third quarter of 2001 to 119.6 per cent five years later (see Figure 5.15). The profit rate has since fallen, but again, the decline is not particularly striking. It was down to 84.1 per cent by the end of 2008, but that was still above the dotcom low. And again it rebounded in Q1 2009, to 98.4 per cent.[40]

—— %, Corporate Profits With Inventory Valuation Adjustment and Capital Consumption Adjustment/Non-Residential Private Fixed Investment

Figure 5.15   US Corporate Profits/Investment

Source: Bureau of Economic Analysis

This does not qualify as the profit rate perhaps in the sense Marx would have identified. A true profit rate is profits vis-à-vis the stock of capital outstanding, rather than the flow of new capital or investment. But there is some ambiguity in Marx's treatment of this issue.[41] And this measure is still instructive since it is based on the flow of new capital. Indeed, as a second order derivative, it is arguably a more sensitive and thus more useful measure of the pressure on profit rates from overaccumulation. Either way, it is still hard to claim from this measure that profit rates have been under pressure.

Looking at domestic profits is an entirely different matter. At the top of the housing boom, more than a third of US company profits were being earned abroad. Indeed, by the fourth quarter of 2008, overseas profits had risen to a record 45.6 per cent of domestic profits (see Figure 5.16). That represented a huge increase over the 5.7 per cent average witnessed during the 1950s and 1960s.[42]

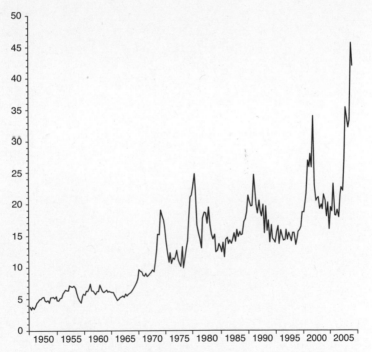

——— %, Corporate Profits With Inventory Valuation Adjustment and Capital Consumption Adjustment Rest of the World/Domestic Industries

Figure 5.16 US Corporate Profits, Rest of the World/Domestic

Source: Bureau of Economic Analysis

Furthermore, a growing share of domestic profits came from the financial sector. During the 1950s and 1960s, an average of 13.1 per cent of domestic profits derived from the finance sector. That grew to a peak of 45.3 per cent in the fourth quarter of 2001 (see Figure 5.17). Finance was responsible for a third of domestic profits at the end of 2006, before the slide in house prices began to take its toll on bank earnings. Even then, finance still accounted for a quarter of domestic profits in Q1 2009, despite the collapse of Lehman Brothers.[43]

The evidence of a profits crisis is compelling when examining domestic companies outside of finance. Again, the ratio of domestic

——— %, Corporate Profits With Inventory Valuation Adjustment and Capital Consumption Adjustment Domestic Non-Financial/Domestic Industries

Figure 5.17   US Domestic Corporate Profits, Non-Financial/Total

Source: Bureau of Economic Analysis

non-financial profits to investment outlays did rise during the housing boom. But the cyclical high of Q3 2006 fell well short of levels seen during much of the post-war period (see Figure 5.18).[44] Indeed, this measure of profit rates only started to fall in earnest during the second half of 1969. But this underlines a key point of the argument articulated by Marxist economists. The decline in profit rates began before the 1980s, and was a precursor to the attack on wages.

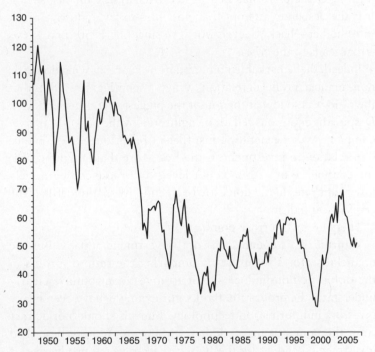

—— %, US Corporate Profits With Inventory Valuation Adjustment and Capital Consumption Adjustment Domestic Non-Financial/Non-Residential Private Fixed Investment

Figure 5.18   US Corporate Profits Domestic Non-Financial/Investment

Source: Bureau of Economic Analysis

In addition, the collapse in profit rates during 2001 is striking and underlines the severity of the crisis that capitalism was already facing following the dotcom boom. It is very easy to be critical of Alan Greenspan and the decision to cut interest rates so aggressively between 2001 and 2003. The criticism is justified in the sense that easy credit never resolved the underlying flaws that precipitated the recession. However, it is not enough to claim that the housing bubble of recent years was solely a function of loose monetary control.

It is worth stressing again that the crisis has not been caused by falling profit rates *per se*. The profit rate does not actually fall until after the crisis has manifested itself in the finance sector. It is the desperate attempt by companies to try and drive profit rates higher – back to levels not seen since the 1950s and 1960s – that leads to the crisis.

Indeed, the remarkable point about the chart showing domestic non-financial profits in relation to investment (Figure 5.18) is that the ratio was so low at the top of the biggest ever housing boom. Despite the enormous reflation engineered by the Federal Reserve, companies were generating insufficient profit outside of finance – in relation to investment in the US. More than anything, it is the confluence of extreme debt levels and these comparatively low profit rates in the domestic real economy that underlines the crisis of capitalism.

There are two further points.

Figure 5.18 is couched in total investment outlays. But the financial sector also invests. Comparing the ratio of profits in the domestic non-finance sector to investment outlays clearly understates the profit rate. Banks, for example, have been heavy investors in information technology. But this should not detract from the points being made here. Marx would have described investment spending by the financial sector as unproductive. It produces no real return. It is divorced from the real economy. Therefore, to look at the ratio of profits among domestic non-financial companies to total investment outlays is arguably still a more effective measure of the 'real' return.

Secondly, the ratio of real investment to GDP rose to a post-war high of 12.7 per cent in the third quarter of 2000. It fell during the dotcom recession, but then rose again to 12.2 per cent in the first quarter of 2008. It is now sliding as the economy tumbles deeper into recession (see Figure 5.19).[45] But for much of the past decade or so, the real rate of investment has been far above the levels sustained during the 1950s and 1960s. This would be seen again as symptomatic of the underlying problem that leads to overproduction, particularly when taken in conjunction with the huge investment in China and other emerging market economies.

—— %, Real Non-Residential Private Fixed Investment/Real GDP

Figure 5.19   US Investment/GDP, Real

Source: Bureau of Economic Analysis

6

A FLAWED ECONOMIC SYSTEM?

Marxist economists have a lot to say about the cause of the 2008 crisis, which deserves scrutiny. Marxists call for a radical political change to the economic system. By contrast, Keynesians are described as reformists. They seek not to change or overthrow the economic system, but merely to improve it. Keynesian prescriptions are designed to work within the existing confines of capitalism.

Indeed, Keynes dismissed Marxism because he believed the free market model was optimal. Keynes argued that 'the solution to the class struggle was not abolition of the market system or private property...but the re-positioning of the financial system to serve the interests of industry and labour'.[1]

Marxists in turn reject much of what Keynes has to say, partly because his policies did not provide a long-term answer to the contradictions of capitalism that lead repeatedly to boom and bust.[2] The tumultuous events of recent years would appear to support such a view.

However, the preponderance of financial crises since the early 1970s is not a refutation of the policies put forward by Keynes. Indeed, failure to adhere to the policies he advocated can also be seen as a contributing factor in the economic downturn that began in 2008.

Globalisation has been cited as one driver of the overaccumulation that precipitated the current economic slump. But the failure to follow Keynes's prescription led to the disastrous inflationary surge of the 1970s and the subsequent political backlash, which in turn provided the intellectual justification for globalisation.

Marxists claim that Keynesian policies ultimately failed, as they were unable to tame stagflation and instead precipitated the sustained attack on organised labour from Reaganomics and Thatcherism. Since these policies ineluctably led to the credit crisis today, Marxists hold Keynesians complicit in allowing the long slide into a potential depression.[3]

However, the inflationary surge of the 1970s was not a failure of 'Keynes'. After his death in 1946, there was a broad retreat from the policies he had supported during the 1930s and through the war.[4] The reversal culminated in a liberalisation of finance that he would surely have opposed. It was certainly contrary to the policies he espoused at Bretton Woods in 1944. By the early 1970s, the monetary reforms of the post-depression years were being systematically dismantled.[5]

Indeed, much of the post-war era was dominated by a 'post-war Keynesian' agenda that bore little resemblance to the economics of Keynes. In the 1945 National Debt Enquiry (NDE), Keynes made it quite clear that any rise in inflation might need to be countered by a reversal of the low interest rate policy.[6]

But this warning was placed at the end of the NDE and that is clearly deliberate. The emphasis of the NDE was on monetary controls, both domestic and external. That would prevent a return to the easy but dear money that prevailed in the late 1920s and led inevitably to the stock market crash. Reversing the policy of low interest rates would be a last resort.

But Keynes was reinvented, and post-war Keynesians placed an exaggerated emphasis on fiscal policy to control the economy and promote full employment. Furthermore, monetary tools and control of the credit system were progressively diluted. Capital flows were liberalised, and a policy of tight but cheap money was replaced by the opposite, which had prevailed before 1929.

Much of this misunderstanding of Keynes's economics has been repeated today by policymakers during the credit crunch. The pursuit of bigger budget deficits to the exclusion of more appropriate monetary tools from 2008 onwards has been contrary to important lessons of the early 1930s. Keynes was first and foremost a monetary economist concerned with getting interest rates down to check the process of debt deflation.[7] His 'primary concern was preventing recession through appropriate monetary policies'.[8]

If policymakers had digested that important lesson today, Western governments might not be saddled with such enormous budget deficits, which are undermining the political support for more aggressive quantitative easing. Indeed, if some of his basic prescriptions had been implemented many countries might never have got into such a mess in the first place. The vast majority of Keynes's contributions to economic theory have long been ignored.[9]

How Long and How Deep?

There is a lot to be gleaned too from Keynes's work in trying to gauge the depth of any downturn and the potential for any recovery. This has indeed been the key reason for the focus on monetary policy in Chapters 2 and 3 of this book. To understand the cause of the recession that began in 2008, it is important to comprehend overaccumulation and the role of globalisation in precipitating this crisis. But it is also critical to evaluate the policy mistakes being made, albeit within the confines of the existing system.

Marx provides a critical understanding of the contradictions within capitalism that brought the world economy to the brink of depression. However, Keynes adds a necessary framework for assessing the threat of a liquidity trap – where it becomes impossible to get borrowing costs down – and by extension the risk of a debt trap, where rising deflation pushes real borrowing costs up. It remains crucial to understanding the duration of this crisis.

Indeed, the US housing market is spiralling downwards and unemployment is soaring because today's policymakers, led by President Obama's adviser Lawrence Summers and Federal Reserve chair Ben Bernanke, have not digested critical lessons of how the tide turned in the early 1930s. Similarly, they along with many others have failed to understand the real cause of Japan's long slump. The policies pursued by the Japanese authorities throughout the 1990s, contravened the advice of Keynes. The same has been true of the US since 2007.

Keynes did have an impact from 1932 onwards in the US and from 1931 onwards in the UK. That is beyond dispute. His policies were an important countervailing force that remains absent today, despite the belated cut in interest rates close to zero. There is only one option left – quantitative easing – and that is in danger of failing too.

Marx did not consider such a solution, but it is recognised by leading Marxist economists that a 'central bank could indeed print money in order to defend against overaccumulation'.[10] However, to analyse the dynamics of the current slump, and understand why it will prove so intractable, it is important to understand liquidity preference and the risk aversion of investors.

Marxists are right in their warning that ultimately it took a world war before full recovery was secured. But as we saw in Chapter 2, the war was financed by extreme policies supported by Keynes. The increased government spending that finally secured full employment was funded by a massive programme of quantitative easing.

And it should be stressed that quantitative easing is not about 'flooding' financial markets with yet more liquidity, as some economists claim. It is meant to be a surgical and nuanced attempt to mitigate the fallout from a devaluation of capital. If there has been overaccumulation of capital, it will be devalued in a crisis.

The point is underlined by events since the collapse of Lehman Brothers and the emergence of huge excess capacity across industry. Allowing short- and long-term interest rates to fall is a necessary palliative. Indeed, low interest rates are part of the recovery mechanism, even in a Marxist framework.

Of course, driving borrowing costs down aggressively as Keynes advocated might delay the necessary destruction of capital that Marxists claim is necessary to secure a lasting recovery. It has to be stressed that zero interest rates and quantitative easing do nothing to resolve the underlying contradictions of capitalism. They do not forestall the risks of more boom and bust.

Nevertheless, Keynes warned that if borrowing costs are not brought down quickly enough, there might not be a recovery. The destruction of capital values would continue for a very long time. The economy would be in a liquidity trap, because borrowing costs had reached a floor. More worryingly, it could then fall into a debt trap as outlined by Irving Fisher, with falling asset prices pushing real borrowing costs up, not down. After all, the Great Depression would have been much worse if *all* borrowing costs had not been forcibly driven lower.

Put another way, the destruction of capital required to restore profitability is not fixed, but is a moving target. In a prolonged recession, profit rates may continue to fall even as capital is written down. There is no natural floor to the devaluation of capital, because there is no limit to deflation. The destruction of capital leads to lower profit rates too as more workers lose their jobs and consumption plummets. A return to higher profit rates is far from automatic.

Therein lies the danger with the repeated attempts to cut wage costs. Employer organisations have been quick to applaud agreements where workers have accepted wage cuts in return for 'job security'. In reality, this does not preserve jobs. In a liquidity trap, central banks are unable to cut borrowing costs any further to mitigate the deflationary impact. Lower wages, therefore, directly increase the risks that other workers will eventually be made redundant, as lower wages drive the economy deeper into recession.

Eventually, profit rates could fall so far that social cohesion is imperilled. Marx certainly warned this was possible. Keynes allows us to evaluate the possibility of such a scenario.

And it is a major risk. Ignoring Keynes has unquestionably amplified the recession. But in turn, there must be a real chance that the conditions for a return to profitable investment may not recur without far-reaching and fundamental changes to the capitalist system.

As we have acknowledged, intervening in a manner outlined by Keynes would have delayed a badly needed recognition that the system needs to change. Cutting interest rates to 1 per cent in 2003 in the US was a case in point. Had the Fed succeeded in stabilising house prices in 2007 or early 2008, it might well have set the stage for another capitalist boom and bust.

The catalogue of policy mistakes made from 2007 onwards leans heavily towards the Marxist view – that it is the system not people that are to blame. Having watched policymakers bring the world economy to the brink of depression, the conclusion is undeniable.

As Marx warned, the inability to understand the true source of the profit renders policymakers unable to see the scale of the underlying crisis. The failure to distinguish between returns from fictitious capital and real value prevents them from acting swiftly. The very nature of the capital accumulation at the top of economic booms, with the huge rise of fictitious capital, and the intoxicating success this brings for many afforded power and influence, blinds them from taking even the basic remedies advocated by Keynes.

It is perhaps worth remembering the exuberance of many during the final months of the bull market. Writing in the *Financial Times* in May 2007, the chief economists from two leading US banks offered their giddy assessment of a global transformation that captured the mood of invincibility. They lauded a

> global awakening that is lifting global living standards by more than any other human endeavour, and the economic liberalisation enabling economies to make more of their scarce resources. Underpinning this development is the integration of half the world's population into the global market economy, and the deepening and broadening of the capital and derivative markets.

And they added, 'Just as the business cycle has lengthened and flattened, so too has the credit cycle… the market has capital for anyone. The only matter for discussion is the price.' They argued, 'The world is going through an economic transformation of historic proportions…creating vast new markets, with enormous opportunities for both business and consumers.' They ended with a rhetorical flourish: 'Why would a more global competitive economy be a detriment to progress?'[11]

Fate, or The System?

Perhaps the last word on this point should be left to the arch-monetarists, Milton Friedman and Anna Schwartz. Along with Keynes, they correctly identified the monetary policy mistakes made during the early 1930s, albeit with the benefit of hindsight, and without giving Keynes the credit for reversing some of these errors. Having examined the Great Depression in considerable detail, they too admitted that the faultline was systemic. But ultimately, Friedman and Schwartz argue that *fate* determined the outcome.

In particular, the premature death of Benjamin Strong, who had been governor of the Federal Reserve Bank of New York from 1914 until 1928, was considered by Friedman, Schwartz and others, to have been a crucial contributor to the Great Depression.

Throughout his tenure at the New York Fed, Strong had been a dominant figure. He 'had the confidence and backing of other financial leaders… the personal force to make his own opinions prevail, and also the courage to act upon them'.[12] In August 1928, just before he died and more than a year before the stock market crash, Mr Strong had warned that a 'breaking point' would necessitate an easy monetary policy, but 'feared the consequences of hesitation or differences of opinion' within the Fed.[13] He was a passionate advocate of quantitative easing and argued that 'if this power were used in a big way, it would stop any panic which might confront us'.[14]

Friedman and Schwartz concluded that 'If Strong had still been alive and head of the New York Bank in the fall of 1930, he would very likely have recognised the oncoming liquidity crisis for what it was, would have been prepared by experience and conviction to take strenuous and appropriate measures to head it off.'[15]

Their assessment has been shared by others, including Irving Fisher, who lamented 'I thoroughly believe that if he [Benjamin Strong] had lived and his policies had been continued, we might have had the stock market crash in a milder form, but after the crash there would not have been the great industrial depression.'[16]

The conclusion of Friedman and Schwartz is telling:

The detailed story of every banking crisis in our history shows how much depends on the presence of one or more outstanding individuals willing to assume responsibility and leadership. *It was a defect of the financial system that it was susceptible to crises resolvable only with such leadership.*[17]

However, they could never bring themselves politically to follow the logic of their important conclusion. And there were few policymakers in 2008, with the exception of David Blanchflower at the Bank of England, who had the courage to voice their fears as the recession loomed. But that is not a fault of individuals, but the system.

7

OBAMA'S CRISIS?

The catalogue of policy mistakes made from the spring of 2007 onwards threatens to magnify the economic slump. In the US, the number of banks in default will rise. Failing to adhere to the basic policy remedies so critical in reversing the Great Depression in 1932, has exposed the Industrialised West to the risk of prolonged economic stagnation. How long will depend on whether governments and central banks – particularly in the US – have the courage to admit their mistakes and shift to more radical solutions.

The Obama administration's attempts to stabilise the housing market had gained little traction by the summer of 2009. It was only five months since the new president moved into the White House. Ordinarily, this was too short a time scale to assess the track record of any new president.

In reality, even at this early stage it was quite clear President Obama was pursuing policies that were little different from those of the Bush era. Indeed, the Obama economic policy was an intensification of the very worst features of the Bush administration. President Bush sought to boost the economy with a tax rebate in the spring of 2008 – supported unequivocally by Obama's economic adviser, Lawrence Summers.[1] Unsurprisingly, the first act of the new president on taking office in January 2009 was to promote an even bigger stimulus.

Fiscal policy did not work under President Bush, and there was no reason to believe it would succeed a second time. Tax rebates in the spring of 2008 provided only a temporary and modest boost to consumption, before it then plunged (see Figure 7.1).[2] But the tax rebates helped drive borrowing costs higher, as the bond market worried about increased issuance of government debt – Treasuries – and fretted over a possible resurgence of inflation.[3] The Bush administration fell foul of an important tenet of Keynes's economics – the absolute necessity of putting monetary policy before fiscal policy.

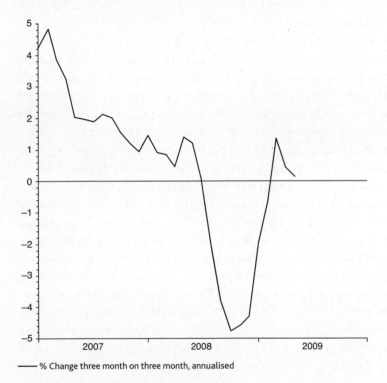

—— % Change three month on three month, annualised

Figure 7.1   US Real Personal Consumption

Source: Bureau of Economic Analysis

None of this has been recognised by Lawrence Summers or President Obama's supporters including economist and *New York Times* columnist, Paul Krugman. Instead, they urged the new president to provide an even bigger fiscal stimulus on assuming the White House. And yet, when the bond market began to express its dislike of the US administration's huge borrowing by driving yields higher and threatening more bank failures, they refused to acknowledge the flaw in their policy advice.[4]

This failed doctrine has many supporters in the academic world. The newest recruit to the Bank of England's Monetary Policy Committee, the American Adam Posen, has long argued that Japan remained mired in economic decline because it did not use fiscal policy enough.[5]

Indeed, it is the collective failing of the US economic establishment to learn the real lessons of Japan's long bear market that is now contributing to a similar, if not worse outcome closer to home. Throughout the 1990s, no US economist was able to offer a credible critique of the repeated policy mistakes witnessed in Japan. Few predicted that Japan would remain in trouble more than a decade later, despite pushing interest rates down to zero and driving its public sector debt burden up nearly threefold.

Nearly 20 years after its bubble burst, Japan is once again being consumed by intense deflation (Figure 7.2).[6] The slide in property prices is accelerating too (Figure 7.3). Indeed, the bear market never even ended despite a boom in the global economy from 2003 onwards. Prices rose in some of the major cities. However, across the country, average property prices have now been falling uninterrupted for more than 17 years, slipping to levels last seen in 1977. From its peak, the Nationwide Land Price index has tumbled 58.5 per cent. A small additional drop of just over 4 per cent would push property prices down to their lowest point since 1973, just before the first oil crisis.[7]

There was, of course, a perfectly logical explanation for Japan's slump. The Bank of Japan was too slow in cutting interest rates. Successive governments then attempted to fill the obvious shortfall in policy stimulus through fiscal measures. It was calamitous. Interest rates never dropped quickly enough, but the cost of borrowing in bond markets fell even more slowly. The government was issuing vast amounts of debt that crowded out the private sector. It can be shown econometrically that the increase in government borrowing drove private sector borrowing costs and bankruptcies higher. The argument has been made in more detail

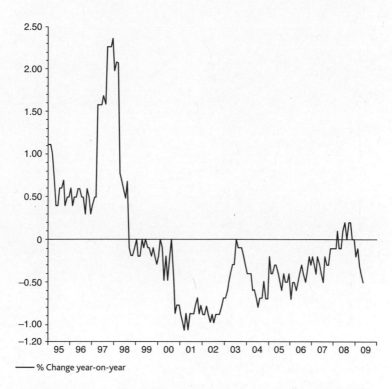

— % Change year-on-year

Figure 7.2   Japan Nationwide Consumer Price Index, Excluding Food and Energy (Core)

Source: Ministry of Internal Affairs and Communication (Japan)

in *Solutions to a Liquidity Trap* and in *The Credit Crunch*. There is no need to rehearse all the points again.[8]

Nevertheless, the poverty of analysis surrounding Japan's economic crisis is disconcerting, because the mistakes are being replicated – on a bigger scale. Already, the budget shortfalls for Fiscal Year 2009 in the US and UK are set to rise above the worst deficit recorded during Japan's bear market.[9]

Furthermore, central banks have run into deeper problems trying to get long-term borrowing costs down.[10] The US and UK may have delivered Japanese-style interest rates – at the short end. But longer-term borrowing costs or bond yields, are proving

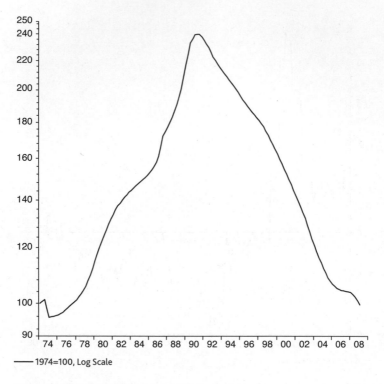

Figure 7.3   Japan Nationwide Land Price Index

Source: Japan Real Estate Institute with Thomson Reuters Datastream calculations

even more difficult to control than in Japan during the 1990s. That in turn is partly a function of the bigger budget deficits in the US and UK.

As we have seen in earlier chapters, it is also due to the innate risk aversion of bond investors that arises when inflation and yields fall to historically low levels. And there is a complicating factor – the large proportion of government debt held overseas.[11] In reality this need not be an obstacle to lower borrowing costs. Those who claim government bond yields cannot fall because foreign investors might sell misunderstand the power of quantitative easing – and economic history. A central bank has the power to control bond yields if it so wishes. Armed with an unlimited balance sheet, it can buy as many government bonds as it wants. The only constraints are a lack of vision and courage. Even the exchange rate risks are over-hyped. When the Bank of England introduced quantitative easing in March 2009, sterling rose, contrary to the expectations of some commentators who fretted over a 'debasement of the currency'. A correct implementation of such a policy can lead to a stronger economy and, therefore, a firmer exchange rate.

If foreign central banks choose to sell US government debt, or Treasuries, this should not matter. The Federal Reserve can simply step into the market, and buy these bonds. Keynes advocated a 'reverse tap', where central banks announce the yield, and by extension the price where it would be prepared to buy any quantity of government bonds.[12] The market could then decide whether it wanted to sell an asset, which – because of the explicit support from a central bank – was suddenly a lot more attractive. In reality, with such an unlimited commitment, there might be surprisingly few sellers. Properly executed the policy could be impressively effective even with a large proportion of debt held overseas.

Breaking Out of the Debt Trap

President Obama will soon realise that the strategy of his advisers is not delivering. He has a number of choices.

He could force the Federal Reserve to adopt the more aggressive policies of reflation seen from 1932 onwards. As we have seen, the Federal Reserve did not reflate willingly on that occasion. It was coerced into taking aggressive action by a Congress increasingly worried about the political consequences of a soaring unemployment rate.

Such a scenario may be unlikely for many reasons, even though it remains eminently feasible. More quantitative easing can in theory drive mortgage rates lower and might eventually stabilise house prices. We can only say *might*. As we have argued before, such a policy would have worked if tried soon enough. But the housing crisis has intensified to the point where arrears are running at record levels. The potential losses will feed directly into pressure for higher lending margins, to rebuild the shattered balance sheets of banks. And that in turn will undermine the efficacy of quantitative easing, because this only works if it succeeds in driving borrowing costs lower.

Indeed, by delaying on quantitative easing, the debt trap had reached a pernicious stage in the US in the summer of 2009. Short-term interest rates were at rock bottom, but banks were hiking lending rates to boost the revenues needed to pay for rising bad debts.

Ominously, US banks had started to raise credit card rates to pay for a sharp increase in the default rate. According to Fitch International, credit card defaults were running at a record 10.4 per cent in the US by the end of June 2009.[13] But higher rates for borrowers will inevitably lead to more write-offs. And with house prices tumbling, the losses incurred by banks when borrowers default will be huge. Increasingly, there is little collateral left when they attempt to claw back debt from card holders.

However, there are huge political obstacles to more aggressive reflation or quantitative easing. Many on the political right see quantitative easing as a ruse to allow governments to avoid taking difficult decisions over soaring budget deficits. Large budget deficits are not sustainable and do not solve the causes of the economic crisis that erupted in 2008. There have been larger deficits during times of war. But these are usually reversed. Wars do not go on forever, partly because they are difficult to finance indefinitely.

But the political right rarely offers a satisfactory alternative, other than to let the market take its natural course, unleashing the forces of 'creative destruction' to deliver a new equilibrium. That can only lead to economic oblivion as the market fails to clear. Once interest rates fall to zero, allowing supply to adjust to a lower demand triggers a downward spiral. In a debt trap, this inability to cut borrowing costs far enough ensures demand falls even more quickly than supply. A race to the bottom ensues, leading ineluctably to a breakdown in social cohesion.

There are other obstacles to a successful reflation strategy similar to that seen in the early 1930s. The widespread shortcomings of policy officials who fail to understand how the most important policy weapon in a central bank's arsenal works have already been detailed. Such a lack of intellectual capacity – particularly within the Federal Reserve – is perhaps the biggest stumbling block to reflation within the confines of the existing system.

Furthermore, a failure to execute quantitative easing effectively and the subsequent near doubling of bond yields has severely impaired the Federal Reserve's credibility in the eyes of the market. A '1932' policy still remains possible, but it would require an even larger open-ended commitment than that needed had the Federal Reserve implemented such a strategy sooner.

Nationalisation of Banks

Soon after President Obama's inauguration, his administration declared its intention to keep banks in the private sector. Obama may have to execute a humbling U-turn. When an economy slides into a debt trap, the market fails. Each bank strives to bolster its balance sheet, but their efforts to 'stay ahead of the curve' drive the whole financial system deeper into the mire. This happens precisely because interest rates have hit a floor.

When interest rates fall during a recession, lending rates usually drop more slowly. The difference is the lending margin and this will tend to rise. It is part of the healing process within a free market. Lending margins are usually compressed during the boom, as banks chase higher market shares. Blind competition at the peak of a bull market or a bubble squeezes the spread between bank funding costs and their lending rates to households and companies. In extreme cases, spreads disappear altogether, as banks try to impress stock market investors and show they are expanding faster than their competitors. Northern Rock was a classic case of this perverse behaviour.

These low spreads are usually inadequate to pay for losses in a recession. However, when central banks cut their lending rates, this provides banks with an opportunity to earn their way out of trouble. As we saw in Chapter 3, the Federal Reserve cut its lending rate by nearly 7 per cent from peak to trough during the Savings and Loan crisis of the late 1980s and early 1990s. The average mortgage rate dropped by less, just under 4 per cent. This widening of lending margins was crucial to the rehabilitation of banks. Not all banks survived even with this considerable support – 745 financial institutions still failed. But the economy did recover.

Ultimately, central banks are engaged in a race against time. The authorities have to cut rates quickly enough to improve bank lending margins *and* stabilise property prices. The fall in central bank rates will reduce bank funding costs. And if banks reduce their lending rates far enough, property prices should stabilise. Central banks have to hope that the higher lending margins help enough banks to pay for their losses. Those that do not either fail or are taken over by the government. But so long as the number of failures and the losses are comparatively modest, the economic system can remain intact.

Of course, there have been numerous bank failures across Europe and the US since late 2006. And the crisis has been much deeper than that of the early 1990s. However, qualitatively it has not been that different from all other previous financial crises over the past century – until now.

The summer of 2009 marks a turning point, when the crisis now threatens to take on a wholly different dimension. Arrears were rising at a record rate in the first three months of 2009 and with unemployment still climbing they were destined to head higher. The implicit losses were climbing even if banks were not admitting to the full scale of the potential hit they might suffer. This assertion is corroborated by the quarterly report from the Federal Financial Institutions Examination Council, which showed a significant *deceleration* in the amount set aside for potential losses, even as arrears posted a record increase (see Figure 7.4).[14]

However, interest rates cannot go negative. As the underlying losses escalate, there is only one option left for banks – higher lending rates to its customers. In a debt trap, that simply leads to more defaults across the banking system. What looks like a

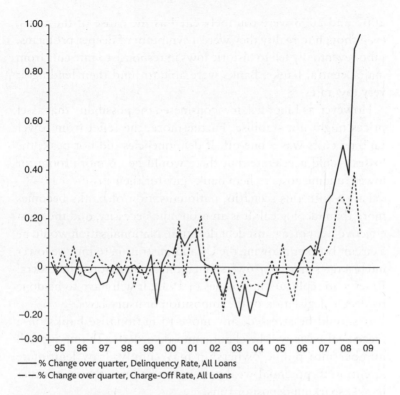

Figure 7.4 US Delinquency and Charge-Off Rates, All Loans

Source: Federal Reserve and Federal Financial Institutions Examination Council

sensible strategy for individual banks, is in aggregate counter-productive. Their collective action ensures the financial system is driven closer to collapse. Once again, the zero bound constitutes a market failure.

This may prove to be a greater problem than even in the early 1930s. In all economic crises since and including the Great Depression, the rehabilitation of banks was facilitated by lower borrowing costs. The US has reached the point where this is no longer possible.

Indeed, it is perhaps ironic that a fall in Libor during the early summer of 2009 was widely interpreted as a sign that banks had turned the corner.[15] The repeated surges in Libor during

2007 and 2008 were routinely cited as the cause of the crisis, even though in reality they were a symptom of deeper problems. Libor eventually fell to historic lows in response to rate cuts from major central banks. Banks were able to fund their lending at very low rates.[16]

However, as Libor fell, few considered the possibility that asset prices might not stabilise. Furthermore, the relief from lower funding costs was a one-off. If delinquencies did not peak, the losses would accelerate, but there would be no more room for lower funding costs to help banks pay for their losses.

Faced with this scenario, nationalisation of banks becomes more than ideological. It is an economic necessity, and the most effective weapon against debt deflation. Nationalisation would be a circuit breaker allowing the US administration to impose lower interest rates on all borrowers. If it is unwilling to force the Federal Reserve to replicate the policies of 1932, it will have to be done by decree, legislation or the imposition of usury laws.

It should be stressed, any move to nationalise banks on a piecemeal basis will be chaotic and disorderly. Taking a small number into public ownership may simply draw legitimate attention to potential weakness in the balance sheets of other banks, sparking depositor runs.

Furthermore, leaving 'healthy' banks in the private sector is dangerous, since their attempts to rebuild lending margins will still compromise the objective of securing reflation. A number of US banks have repaid funds to the US administration in the summer of 2009 claiming they were solvent.

Whether they were sound was immaterial. As we have already seen from the Federal Financial Institutions Examination Council, the US banking system was struggling in Q1 2009 to cover its potential losses and failing to increase its charge-off rate in line with arrears. Stronger banks may be able to foreclose more aggressively and 'get ahead' for a short while. However, the zero bound ensures this can only be done at the expense of driving property prices down further, triggering additional defaults as more borrowers slip into negative equity. This is not creative destruction, but an intensification of the debt trap.

Nationalisation Not Enough

Nationalisation is far from a panacea and should be seen as merely a stepping stone. The UK bank Northern Rock was taken into public ownership in September 2007. By the first half of 2008, it was repossessing far more homes than other banks.[17] And a year later, it is still posting heavy losses. In its own right, nationalisation solves little.[18]

Public ownership allows governments to deliver the monetary policy central banks are unable or unwilling to deliver. Governments will be able to dictate borrowing rates. Left in the private sector, banks will not cut lending rates because they are trying to pay for their losses. After cuts in borrowing costs for households and consumers have been unilaterally imposed upon them by government, banks will initially receive smaller revenues as their lending margins shrink. But driving these borrowing costs down will also reduce the debt write-offs or losses, which are multiples of their lending margins.

The US lender Fannie Mae provides a good example of the problem. It reported a near doubling of its revenues or lending margins during the first three months of 2009, compared with the same period in 2008. The Federal Reserve had slashed interest rates to 0.25 per cent, allowing the nationalised lender to raise margins on its mortgages. But the losses from defaulting homeowners climbed more than sixfold.[19] The boost from rock bottom interest rates was overwhelmed by the pace of deflation. Net losses jumped tenfold to $23.2 billion, leading to yet another bailout from the US taxpayer.

This one example, from a lender responsible for 26 per cent of all US mortgages, underlined the futility of current policies. But it also shows that nationalisation is not enough. Fannie Mae had been under *de facto* government control throughout the bull market. It was under the US administration's complete control after 7 September 2008. The Obama administration also persuaded Fannie Mae to introduce another moratorium. And the losses still multiplied.[20]

But it has been unwilling to use its control over Fannie Mae – and the other giant nationalised lender, Freddie Mac – to change its policy substantively. That is partly because the Obama administration is wedded to a private sector solution.

There is a deeper problem. Instructing Fannie Mae and Freddie Mac to impose different borrowing costs and adopting an even longer moratorium on its loans is pointless with the majority of lenders still in the private sector. These other banks would be free to foreclose aggressively, pushing property prices lower and driving up the losses for the state controlled banks higher. They would still be dumping their losses onto the taxpayer.

In short, nationalisation only works in a debt trap if every bank is controlled by the US authorities with a view to cutting all borrowing costs for homeowners and companies, and imposing a nationwide moratorium, perhaps for one or two years. The imposition of lower borrowing costs would have to extend to mortgage bond holders too, by decree. The legal rights of these bond investors will have to be overridden.[21]

The debt trap is not unsolvable. Even if property prices are sliding and unemployment is rising, there will be a particular level of debt servicing costs or borrowing rates that will eventually ensure equilibrium for property markets. Nobody can be sure where that level of borrowing costs lies. But it will exist, and can be imposed by state control and intervention.

And the short-run losses to state-owned banks from lower mortgage rates will in the long run be comfortably outweighed by the gains from preventing an endless procession of bad debts. Should the US administration still be inclined to return banks to the private sector, it may even find that it could secure a positive return that would help to pay (in part) for the losses incurred from the disastrous policies pursued from 2007 onwards. Whether the US administration should be so inclined is a necessary debate in itself. A more important task will be the creation of lending and capital controls that will permit a policy of cheap but tight money, to avoid a re-run of the past three decades or more of loose monetary conditions.

Writing Debts Off?

A number of commentators have continued to argue for debt write-offs, forbearance or even deeper capital injections from the taxpayer as an alternative solution. This is fraught with far bigger risks, and likely to fail.[22]

Such a policy is regarded as less extreme than outright nationalisation of an entire financial system. It is seen as a nuanced, surgical policy designed to remove problem debts and recapitalise struggling banks. The authorities in effect act as a catalyst for a process of creative destruction that has been stalled by a refusal of banks to recognise the scale of the debt crisis. Banks need to 'confess' their losses, mark all assets to realistic and lower valuations. The cycle of debt deflation will then come to a natural conclusion, it is claimed.

Japan is often invoked as an example of the dangers in refusing to acknowledge the true losses sitting on the balance sheets of banks. The analogy usually cited is the infamous collapse of Yamaichi Securities in November 1997, which had hidden more than ¥200 billion of losses for six years.[23]

It is a flawed theory. The real cause of Japan's long bear market from 1990 was the failure to get borrowing costs down and the wrong implementation of loose fiscal policy as a substitute.[24] Banks and brokers were sitting on their losses, but that begs the question of what caused them to multiply in the first place. Recognising losses sooner and disposing of them is not painless. Indeed, it was the fire-sale of repossessed properties through auction houses from the early 1990s onwards that triggered a further slide in land prices, bringing down yet more banks. Critically, monetary policy was ineffective in countering the deflation created by the losses that were recognised.[25]

Thus simply writing down all loans to realistic valuations is not a resolution. If US banks had written down their losses in the first three months of 2009 in line with the surge in arrears, it would have been more 'honest'.[26]

But the real problem lies with the inadequate policy response by the authorities, who are in full possession of the facts. They have connived with banks. By allowing them to slow the rate of increase in their charge-off rate in the first three months of 2009, banks were able to post better profit reports that did not reflect the true scale of the crisis facing the residential and commercial property markets. It was a desperate ploy by the Obama administration and Federal regulators, an attempt to ramp bank share prices in a bid to persuade investors that the strategy for reflation was succeeding. However, they have done this because they are unwilling to countenance a necessary shift in policy beyond traditional parameters.

8

BREAKING WITH THE PAST

Each and every financial crisis will always give rise to a struggle between employers and workers. The shakeout in the labour market has already been brutal, particularly in the US. There is every chance that the official jobless rate will jump to levels not seen since the early 1930s. On the wider U6 measure, it is already there.

But there will be several differences. Governments and central banks were successful in creating an economic recovery in the early 1930s. Unemployment did eventually fall. It may not have been quick, and the scourge of mass unemployment afflicted both the US and UK throughout the 1930s. Nevertheless, the downward drift in the jobless rates did provide some hope amidst the despair.

Furthermore, the Marx critique that the crisis of 2008 was caused by overaccumulation implies that there has to be an extended period of 'traumatic devaluation' before any recovery can take hold. Globalisation has generated greater overinvestment than in the late 1920s, because so many emerging market countries have been used by the West as an extension of the domestic production base. This in itself creates bigger risks for workers. A similar point can also be made about the emergence of extreme levels of fictitious capital.

But these are still only risks. The reality of how far unemployment rises will also be governed by the lack of policy flexibility. Having spent so much money trying to rescue banks and causing their budget deficits to explode, Western governments now have less room to cushion the fallout from persistent unemployment. Nowhere is that more true than in the US and UK. If these economies relapse in 2010, the deficits could rise above 15 per cent of GDP.

In the US, Republicans now charge Obama with fiscal profligacy (Figure 8.1). Following their defeat in November 2008, they are regrouping around the banner of fiscal conservatism. Under Bush, they supported three major tax-cutting initiatives, huge increases in military spending and then a final last throw of the die to save the economy – a tax rebate in the spring of 2008. That still failed to stem the slide into recession. No matter, now they are in opposition further spending increases are being resisted (Figure 8.2).

—— $ Billion, 12 month moving total

Figure 8.1   US Federal Government Budget Balance

Source: Department of the Treasury

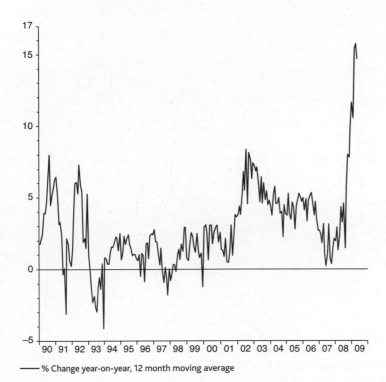

———— % Change year-on-year, 12 month moving average

Figure 8.2   US Federal Government Outlays, Adjusted by Consumer Price Index

Source: Department of the Treasury

In the UK, the Labour government has been accused by opposition parties of being careless too, failing to rein in public spending, which they claim has caused the deficit to rise so quickly during the downturn (Figure 8.4). In reality, the rise in public sector borrowing has almost entirely been driven by a collapse in tax revenues (Figure 8.5). Indeed, spending remained under remarkable control for an economy in the midst of its worst post-war recession (Figure 8.6).

Nevertheless, public sector employees were expected to take their share of the pain, since workers in the private sector were being forced to accept pay cuts to 'preserve jobs'. The logic was

Figure 8.3   US Federal Government Receipts, Adjusted by Consumer Price Index

Source: Department of the Treasury

perverse. Keynes warned against attacking wages during the Great Depression. This was an important message in _The General Theory of Employment, Interest and Money._[1]

However, the futility of cutting wages is magnified by the proximity of the zero bound for interest rates. As we saw in Chapter 4, ordinarily a fall in wages would be countered by interest rate cuts. But the credit crunch and the tardy response have left central banks with much less room to cushion the fallout from wage cuts.

The utter failure to follow Keynes's prescription in the US and UK can also be seen by comparing the deteriorating fiscal position today with the increase in government spending witnessed during

— £ Billion, 12 month moving total

Figure 8.4   UK Public Sector, Total Net Borrowing

Source: Office for National Statistics

the Second World War. On this occasion, the budget deficit rose to a peak of 28.1 per cent of GDP in the US and 26.1 per cent of GDP in the UK, securing full employment.[2] The deficits could be at least half of these levels in 2010, yet unemployment may be climbing and house prices still on the slide, particularly in the US. There will be precious little to show for the money. Socialising the losses of the banking crisis will undermine the ability of governments to respond to a prolonged economic crisis.

The precise impact of the New Deal implemented by the Roosevelt administration in the early 1930s has been the subject of debate over the years. However, one point is beyond dispute. When President Roosevelt took power, the budget deficit was

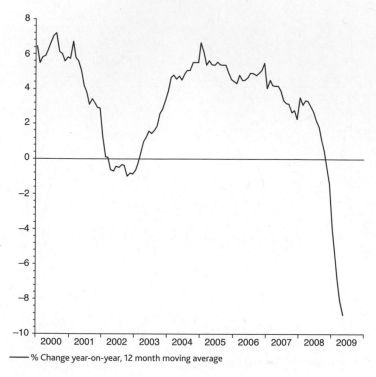

Figure 8.5   UK Central Government, Current Receipts, Adjusted by
Consumer Price Index

Source: Office for National Statistics

small. Under the previous Hoover administration, monetary policy
had been the primary weapon to try to stabilise the economy. It
was meeting with some success.

As we have seen, contrary to popular assertion, the recovery
did not begin under President Roosevelt, but instead came from
Congressional pressure exerted on the Federal Reserve during
President Hoover's tenure. And the budget deficit was still only
4.7 per cent of GDP in 1932, the final year of Hoover's administration. The peak deficit during the Great Depression was 5.1
per cent of GDP, in 1934.[3] This was a policy sequence more in
line with Keynes's remedy, with monetary tools to the forefront
and fiscal measures secondary.

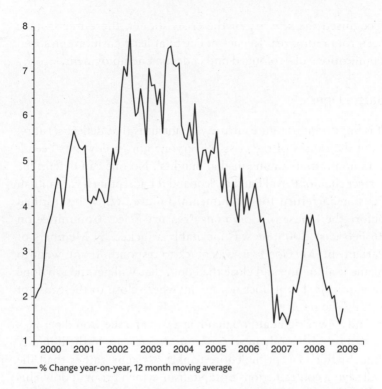

Figure 8.6   UK Central Government, Current Expenditure, Adjusted by
Consumer Price Index

Source: Office for National Statistics

The war experience is illustrative too. The governments ran up
huge deficits for the duration of the war, but these then fell once
the national crisis was over. Having secured full employment on
the back of massive increases in spending, reducing the deficit did
not suddenly lead to job losses. Factories were switched back to
producing consumer goods. After years of rationing, there was huge
pent-up demand. The fiscal boost that delivered full employment
could be unwound without creating a new jobs crisis.

Such an outcome seems impossible to imagine now that today's
policymakers have made such errors attempting to resolve the
banking crisis. If they had not been so ideologically opposed
to nationalisation of banks – particularly in the US – and had

recognised the severity of the crisis sooner, there might have been room for a real Keynes policy to at least cushion the social ramifications of prolonged and endemic unemployment.

Battle Lines

It is important to refute an array of untruths that deflect scrutiny from the causes of the crisis. 'Everyone got greedy' has been a common refrain among media 'pundits'. No one can defend the former chair of Royal Bank of Scotland for accepting a gargantuan pension in return for monumental failure. When he testified before the House of Commons Treasury Select Committee on 26 February 2009, he was inevitably attacked by Members of Parliament. Mr Goodwin was quick to respond: 'If you want to blame it all on me and close the book, that will get the job done very quickly, but it does not go anywhere close to the cause of all this', he retorted.[4]

And he was right, although not in a way that he would perhaps recognise. Mr Goodwin was, of course, referring to the liquidity crunch which swept the entire banking system, rather than the underlying contradictions of capitalism, which brought down his and many other banks.

It is absolutely correct to protest against rewards for failure and call for a radical change in the banking system. But nationalisation is a necessary but far from sufficient step towards economic recovery. A more important change is democratic accountability and representation across a far broader section of society, to attack the vested interests of big business that led to the credit crisis.

With unemployment rising, politicians and trade union leaders have been loath to rock the boat and criticise large corporations. Indeed, the more profitable companies are seeking to strengthen their stranglehold, with little opposition from politicians, claiming their expansion into new markets would create jobs. Tesco's announcement in the spring of 2009 that it planned to 'more than double in size' was thus met with barely a murmur.[5]

But the relentless expansion of large corporations will merely reinforce an important dynamic that contributed so much to the crisis of 2008. The '300 biggest companies own one quarter of all productive assets worldwide and control more than half of the world market in consumer durables, steel, airlines, electronics, oil, computers, media, aerospace and cars'.[6]

Globalisation has been driven by large corporations. They in turn have continued to grow because of globalisation. It has been a mutually reinforcing dynamic. It is large corporations that have enjoyed the power to outsource and roam the globe, seeking out cheaper production bases, abusing 'free trade' to drive down labour costs. It is large corporations that are responsible – indirectly – for the explosion of credit and the housing bubbles that were so necessary to ensure any economic growth after the collapse of the dotcom bubble.

But these 'monopolies', as we have seen already, are driven to invest overseas by the contradictions of capitalism. Falling profit rates at home led corporations to seek out alternative markets to expand margins. They represent the ultimate manifestation of the problem Marx identified with capitalism. Indeed, Lenin took Marx's analysis one step further, equating the emergence of monopolies as the 'quintessence of imperialism'.

Monopolies grew out of free trade, but their breathless expansion has sown the seeds of decay. They have pushed the contradictions of capitalism to the point where free trade itself may eventually be imperilled by persistently high unemployment.

Protectionism will not solve the underlying contradictions with capitalism that led to the economic slump. It will not reverse the grip of big business. Protectionism has spread its tentacles too deep to be thwarted now by a rise in import tariffs or duties, neither of which fundamentally addresses the imbalance between capital and labour.

That can only come from a reversal of the shareholder model that denies a democratic voice to workers. Decisions taken ostensibly in the interests of shareholders do not even benefit investors. As we saw with Burberry and many others, the race to the bottom ultimately destroys share prices too. By the summer of 2009, stock markets in both the US and the UK were lower than in 1999, when the markets were swept by dotcom mania.[7] In real terms, the performance of stock markets has been even more abysmal, particularly in the UK (Figures 8.7 and 8.8). Investors would have been better off leaving their money on deposit, earning low rates of interest, dispensing with the cost and anxiety of investing in a stock market that is unable to climb.

January 1990=100

Figure 8.7   Dow Jones Industrials Adjusted by Consumer Price Index

Source: Thomson Reuters Datastream and Bureau of Labor Statistics

Decisions taken at the corporate board no longer reflect the interests of the wider community or the best interests of the economy. Company executives are unable and unwilling to countenance the environmental impact of their commercial activities too. The shareholder model has become a destructive medium, undermining communities, social cohesion and the ability of governments to fund public services. Unchallenged, the

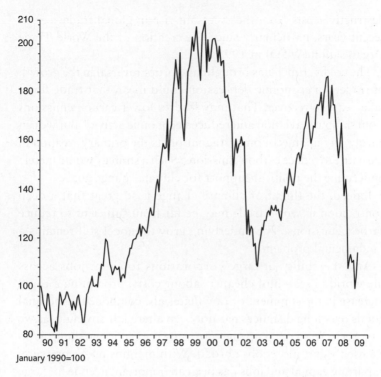

January 1990=100

Figure 8.8   FTSE 100 Price Index Adjusted by Consumer Price Index

Source: Thomson Reuters Datastream and Office for National Statistics

collapse of this asset bubble may lead to the deepest reversal in the provision of public services in the post-war era.

Democratic accountability can only be injected into corporations through direct representation of all those with a common interest. Worker representatives are not a new concept. Nevertheless, a revolution in the structure of 'business', away from shareholder value towards community goals – employment, social stability and the environment – is more critical than ever.

Climate Change

For some years, climate change has cast doubts on the validity of the current thrust of globalisation. There have been huge destructive costs from the incessant rise in global trade seen in recent years, particularly since the creation of the World Trade Organisation (WTO) in 1995.

The credit crunch has brought an abrupt reversal in the growth of trade. An economic depression could mean that trade flows take years to recover. That may lead to lower carbon emissions from shipping, aviation and reduced economic activity. But we can hardly rely upon economic stagnation as the primary weapon in the battle to reduce carbon emissions. Such a strategy would merely undermine the political support for climate change goals.

Indeed, the threat of climate change is so great that a deep contraction in world trade may be far from sufficient to reduce carbon emissions. The underlying growth model still remains a fundamental problem.

And the ability of large corporations to shunt jobs across the world in search of cheaper labour costs, prompting a rapid increase in the shipment of raw materials, components and final goods over long distances has not been altered. If anything, as we have seen, Western companies are using the economic slump as an excuse to shift more jobs abroad. With margins under pressure, exporting capital and jobs has been an important avenue for large businesses to restore profitability.

A second problem is technological change. Economic slumps will reduce spending on research and development. Technological progress may slow, but it will not cease. And with the current construct of globalisation, there remains a worrying potential for innovations to be used to accelerate the rise in carbon emissions.

Rapid improvements in manufacturing efficiency, aided by new production techniques will continue to drive down the cost of aircraft production. Individual planes may be more fuel efficient, but lower production costs will make outsourcing more viable. Gains from lower carbon emissions per aircraft may then be offset by a renewed, rapid expansion in the growth of aviation cargo.

Indeed, the impact on the production of aircraft in the US has been quite limited during the economic downturn thus far. Even allowing for the longer lags in this industry, it is instructive to see that aircraft production had fallen by an average of just 1.7 per cent y/y in the first five months of 2009. That compares with a drop of 14.3 per cent y/y across the entire manufacturing sector over the corresponding period.[8]

A similar point must be made for shipping, a significantly underestimated source of carbon emissions.[9] Shipping rates have collapsed because of a surplus of vessels (see Figure 8.9). The production of ships rose sharply just as the boom came to an end. Suddenly, it makes even more 'economic' sense for corporations to seek cheaper wages across the globe. In short, a sudden glut and surfeit of aircraft and ships have enhanced the raw economics of globalisation.

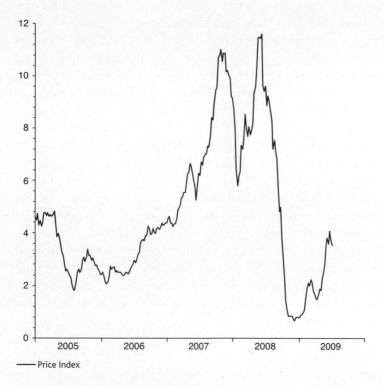

— Price Index

Figure 8.9   Baltic Exchange Dry Index

Source: Thomson Reuters Datastream

The pressure on governments to create jobs in the midst of a depression may add further impetus to the dispersion of jobs and trade, undermining carbon emission targets. The promise of 60,000 new jobs was used as a cynical justification for the expansion of Heathrow airport. Business leaders warned that without the third runway, jobs would be lost. Union leaders capitulated to the government's arm twisting, meekly supporting the proposed airport expansion which makes a mockery of climate change goals.

Job creation does not have to be met by environmentally destructive projects that underpin the expansion of global trade. Indeed, if governments were so determined to apply a Keynes stimulus, they could have focused their investment on alternative energy, green technology and carbon-reduction infrastructure projects. This would be a more appropriate application of quantitative easing – using a central bank's balance sheet to invest in industries that reduce carbon emissions while creating jobs too. The balance sheets of central banks were used to fund a huge expansion of the military in the late 1930s and early 1940s. Such a strategy could be employed for climate change goals today.

President Obama did identify alternative energy as a target for increased spending in his administration's first budget. But the increased spending was still a small proportion of the resources being made available for bank rescues and tax rebates that do not even work anyway.

The threat of climate change underlines the need for a radical shift away from the shareholder model. A drive towards greater representation need not reject the benefits that come from trade. The challenge will be to create a new world economic order that preserves some of the gains from trade where genuine comparative advantage exists, but eliminates many of the destructive features of globalisation.

A new world economic order has to recognise that the relentless growth in trade volumes over long distances is neither environmentally sustainable, nor economically sensible. Much of this growth in trade since the creation of the WTO has been driven by the pursuit of lower labour costs.

Governments also have to exert greater control over corporations to eliminate pointless, wasteful trade flows. It is an obvious point that governments in the US and UK have turned a blind eye to the surge in cheap imports as outsourcing proliferated, thus allowing both countries to incur enormous record trade deficits. Bubble countries have been the worst offenders, experiencing huge increases in the shipment of imports, as their domestic industries were shut down and then relocated.

If we are serious about combating the catastrophic rise in carbon emissions, the limits to the free market need to be recognised quickly. The contradictions of capitalism did not just create the credit crunch. They lie at the root of rising carbon emissions. In a world where productivity has never been higher, it is unconscionable that the planet should be imperilled. Marx might not have imagined the transformation in productivity that has occurred since his death in 1883. But he would have recognised the failure of the world to translate these improvements into a *sustainable* standard of living. We are more productive than ever, but many in the West work longer hours, because of competition and the shareholder model.

The challenge posed by many of these issues, from democratic accountability, worker representation, rebalancing of corporate power and climate change, cannot be ignored. But the danger remains that the radical changes needed to our political economy will be derailed by the policy failings articulated in this book.

NOTES

Introduction

1 Source: Department of Commerce, Bureau of Economic Analysis. Between December 2008 and May 2009, Disposable Personal Income (annualised rate) rose $465.2 billion, or 4.4 per cent. Personal Incomes rose by $176.9 billion, or 1.5 per cent. The difference of $288.3 billion, or 2.7 per cent, was a measure of the boost to Disposable Personal Income from lower taxes. In addition, Government Social Benefits to Persons rose $317.1 billion (annualised rate) or 16.8 per cent between December 2008 and May 2009. These two combined show that the personal sector received a boost of $605.4 billion (annualised rate) in the first five months of 2009.

Both of these boosts to Personal Disposable Income helped to stimulate retail sales, excluding gasoline and autos, by 1.3 per cent m/m in January 2009 and 0.8 per cent m/m in February 2009. But retail sales on this 'core' measure then fell 0.9 per cent m/m in March, 0.1 per cent m/m in April before rising 0.1 per cent m/m in May. A similar pattern was observable for Personal Consumption Expenditures. Consumption rose 0.7 per cent m/m in January 2009, was unchanged in February, fell 0.2 per cent in March, dropped 0.1 per cent in April before rising 0.2 per cent in May.

2 Source: RealtyTrac. Foreclosure filings, including default notices, auction sale notices and bank repossessions, were reported on 341,180 properties in March 2009, 342,038 in April and 321,480 in May. The RealtyTrac data only extends back to January 2005 but these were record months, and were up 46.0 per cent y/y, 40.6 per cent y/y and 23.1 per cent y/y respectively.

3 See 'Lenders Voluntarily Delaying Majority of Scheduled Foreclosures', 17 June 2009, www.thetruthaboutmortgage.com/lenders-voluntarily-delaying-majority-of-scheduled-foreclosures/, accessed 2 July 2009.

4 Source: Bureau of Labor Statistics. Employed, Non-Farm Industries, Total, fell 467,000 in June 2009. In the early 1980s, 431,000 jobs were lost at the worst point (May 1980). In the early 1990s, 306,000 jobs were lost at the worst point (February 1991). And during the dotcom recession, 325,000 jobs were lost in October 2001.

5 Source: Department of Commerce, Office for National Statistics, Eurostat. In Q1 2009, real Gross Domestic Product (GDP) fell 2.5

per cent y/y in the US, 4.9 per cent y/y in the UK and 4.8 per cent y/y in Euroland (EA 16). The decline in US GDP was not the worst in the post-Second World War era, yet. Real GDP dropped 3.0 per cent y/y in Q1 1950. But a decline in Q2 would ensure that this was the longest post-war contraction. And because real GDP rose 0.7 per cent q/q in Q2 2008, any drop in Q2 2009 would ensure this was also the steepest post-war contraction. In the UK, the Q1 2009 decline was the steepest in the post-war era. In Euroland, it was the steepest since comparable records began in Q1 1996.

6   Source: People's Bank of China. Financial Institution Loans rose 27.1 per cent y/y in April 2009, compared with 15.9 per cent y/y in December 2008. See 'Lending surge alarms Beijing', *The Nikkei*, 23 April 2009.

7   See 'Wary banks hobble toxic asset plan', *Wall Street Journal*, 29 June 2009.

8   Belatedly recognising that its plan was not working, the Obama administration announced on 29 June 2009 that homeowners with 25 per cent negative equity would be allowed to participate in the Making Home Affordable Refinance Program.

9   See 'A game of credit cost smoke and mirrors at Wells Fargo', HousingWire.Com, 9 April 2009, www.housingwire.com/2009/04/09/credit-cost-smoke-at-mirrors-at-wells-fargo/, accessed 7 July 2009. See also 'Congress helped banks defang key rule', *Wall Street Journal*, 3 June 2009.

10   Source: S&P/Case-Shiller, Home Price Index, 10-City Composite. Between June 2006 and April 2009, the 10-City Composite index fell 33.6 per cent. A drop of 60 per cent from this high would take the 10-City Composite index down to the level seen in February 1999. A 70 per cent decline would take the 10-City Composite down to levels last seen in July 1987.

11   Source: Federal Reserve, Flow of Funds. Real Estate Assets, Households, fell from a high of $21.882 trillion in Q4 2006 to $17.870 trillion in Q4 2008, a drop of $4.012 trillion.

12   See Joint Statement by the Treasury, FDIC, OCC, OTS and the Federal Reserve, Board of Governors of the Federal Reserve System press release, 23 February 2009, www.federalreserve.gov/newsevents/press/bcreg/20090223a.htm, accessed 3 July 2009. 'Because our economy functions better when financial institutions are well managed in the private sector, the strong presumption of the Capital Assistance Program is that banks should remain in private hands.'

13   See 'Volcker makes a comeback as part of Obama brain trust', *Wall Street Journal*, 21 October 2008. See also 'US wants to keep banks

private in new rescue plan', *USA Today*, 23 February 2009, www.usatoday.com/money/industries/banking/2009-02-23-bank-rescue_N.htm, accessed 3 July 2009.

14 G. Turner, *The Credit Crunch*, Pluto Press, 2008.

Chapter 1

1 G. Turner, *The Credit Crunch*, Pluto Press, 2008, pp. 188–9.

2 Source: The Mortgage Lender Implode-O-Meter, www.ml_implode.com, accessed 28 April 2009. JP Morgan offered $2 a share for Bear Stearns on 17 March 2008. At that point, 238 mortgage companies had ceased trading.

3 Ben Bernanke, 'The Crisis and the Policy Response', The Stamp Lecture, London School of Economics, 13 January 2009.

4 Source: *Historical Statistics of the United States, Colonial Times to 1970, Part 2*, US Department of Commerce, Bureau of the Census, 1975, p. 992. The M2 measure of money supply contracted 1.9 per cent y/y in 1930 and then 6.6 per cent y/y in 1931. These early declines were followed by bigger falls of 15.6 per cent y/y and 10.6 per cent y/y in 1932 and 1933 respectively. See also M. Friedman & A.J. Schwartz, *A Monetary History of the United States, 1867–1960*, Princeton University Press, 1963, pp. 166–7 and 311. Ironically, the relatively new existence of the Federal Reserve may have contributed to this failure in the early 1930s. In previous banking crises, notably in 1907, stronger banks had typically taken the lead when liquidity problems arose. The new Federal Reserve system, which had only been created in 1921, provided an 'escape mechanism' for larger banks should they run into trouble. They no longer felt obliged to step in to support smaller banks. In 1907, the intervention of larger banks had been a crucial mechanism for easing the liquidity crisis.

5 Friedman & Schwartz, *A Monetary History of the United States*, pp. 308–9.

6 See 'Subprime mortgage bond risks surge, index suggests', Bloomberg, 8 February 2007 and 'HSBC says US loan defaults will hit profits', *Guardian*, 9 February 2007.

7 See 'Losing Ground: Foreclosures in the Subprime Market and Their Cost to Homeowners', Center for Responsible Lending, December 2006. See also Turner, *The Credit Crunch*, pp. 58–9.

8 Source: Federal Reserve, Flow of Funds (FoF), F.218. Home Mortgages – Issuers of Asset-Backed Securities, Annualised.

9 Source: Federal Reserve, FoF, F.218 Home Mortgages – Issuers of Asset-Backed Securities, Annualised, fell from a peak of $634.1 billion in Q3 2005 to $616.4 billion in Q4 2005. It then fell to

$570.0 billion in Q1 2006, rose to $575.8 billion in Q2 2006, dropped again to $520.4 billion in Q3 2006 and $388.7 billion in Q4 2006. The figures for 2007 are $349.9 billion, $281.4 billion, –$231.2 billion and –$264.5 billion respectively in Q1, Q2, Q3 and Q4. For 2008, issuance was –$269.3 billion, –$346.5 billion, –$313.1 billion, –$353.5 billion over the four consecutive quarters. And in Q1 2009, issuance was –$332.0 billion.

10   Source: Federal Reserve, FoF, BEA and *Historical Statistics of the United States, Colonial Times to 1970, Part 2*, pp. 224, 992. The contraction in mortgage-backed securities during Q3 2007 was equal to a drop of 1.7 per cent of GDP. The drop in M2 during 1930 was equal to 0.9 per cent of GDP. It is true that M2 did not contract in 2006 or 2007. However, by then, it had become a little followed measure of credit, much of which had migrated far beyond the narrow domain of money supply aggregates. For the record, M2 rose 5.4 per cent y/y in December 2006 and 5.6 per cent y/y in December 2007.

11   Friedman & Schwartz, *A Monetary History of the United States, 1867–1960*, p. 358.

12   Source: Bureau of Labor Statistics (BLS), Office for National Statistics (ONS) and Eurostat.

13   See 'What if the Bank has lost its magic?', Stephen King, *Independent*, 30 June 2008. 'Their [emerging markets] interest rates are low, their inflation rates are rising, their economies are overheating, and their resulting excessive demand for commodities is leaving the rest of us with a higher bill for food and energy.'

14   Source: Goldman Sachs Commodity Price Index, and Thomson Reuters Datastream for Spot Brent Crude Oil. In truth, from a longer perspective, the peak for base metals came on 4 May 2007. The peak on 5 March 2008 was 3.5 per cent below the 4 May 1997 high.

15   Source: Goldman Sachs Commodity Price Index.

16   Source: Goldman Sachs Non-Energy Commodity Price Index and Thomson Reuters Datastream. Total commodity prices peaked on 3 July 2008. The Non-Energy Commodity Price Index peaked on 12 March 2008.

17   Source: BLS and ONS. There was clear evidence of a real wage squeeze. US Average Hourly Real Earnings, Private Non-Farm Industries fell 2.4 per cent y/y in July 2008. UK Average Earnings Index Whole Economy Including Bonus, adjusted by the CPI, dropped 0.8 per cent y/y in July 2008.

18   Source: BLS, ONS and Eurostat. In the US, Average Hourly Earnings, Private Non-Farm Industries, eased from a 2007 peak of 4.2 per cent y/y in July, to 3.8 per cent y/y by August 2008. Indeed, it is

remarkable to note that this measure of nominal wage rates has still not been above 4.5 per cent y/y since April 1983. In the UK, the Average Earnings Index Whole Economy Including Bonus slowed from a 2007 high of 4.5 per cent y/y (three months to February of that year) to 3.4 per cent y/y during the three months to August 2008. Excluding Bonus, the 2007 peak for Average Earnings Index Whole Economy was just 3.7 per cent y/y in the three months to August and the three months to September. It slowed fractionally to 3.6 per cent y/y in the three months to August 2008. In Euroland, there was more evidence of an uptick in wages. Hourly labour costs: Indicator of Negotiated Wages, accelerated from 2.1 per cent y/y in Q4 2007 to 3.6 per cent y/y in Q4 2008. When adjusted by the CPI, the negotiated wage rate still shrank in real terms, falling 0.1 per cent y/y in 2008, compared with no change in 2007.

19 For a longer explanation of this critical cause of the credit bubble, see Turner, *The Credit Crunch*, Chapter 4, '"Free Trade" and Asset Bubbles', pp. 48–83.

20 See Turner, *The Credit Crunch*, pp. 95–106.

21 Source: BLS and ONS. US CPI, All Items, Less Food & Energy. In the early 1980s, this peaked at 13.6 per cent y/y in June 1980. In the early 1990s, it peaked at 5.6 per cent y/y in February 1991. It also reached a cyclical high of 2.9 per cent y/y in September 2006. The 2008 peak of 2.5 per cent y/y came in January, July, August and September. The UK CPI, Excluding Energy, Food, Alcohol and Tobacco, peaked at 2.2 per cent y/y in September 2008. The CPI data begins in January 1996. The Retail Price Index All Items Excluding Mortgage Interest (RPIX) is not strictly comparable, but it peaked at 20.8 per cent y/y in May 1980 and 9.5 per cent y/y in October 1990. The RPIX peaked at 5.5 per cent y/y in September 2008.

22 Source: Eurostat. Core inflation is CPI, Excluding Energy, Food, Energy, Alcohol and Tobacco.

23 Source: BLS, ONS and Eurostat. In the US, CPI, Airline Fares, accelerated to 20.9 per cent y/y in August 2008. In the UK, CPI, Passenger Transport by Air climbed to 26.6 per cent y/y in September 2008. In Euroland, it accelerated to 17.3 per cent y/y in August 2008.

24 See 'Tesco targets Aldi and Lidl', *Financial Times*, 17 September 2008. 'M&S's profits tumble as consumers tighten belts', *Independent*, 28 September 2008. 'Credit crisis helps Aldi sales head for £2bn', *Independent*, 7 November 2008. 'Upmarket customers help boost sales at Asda', *Independent*, 14 November 2008. 'It is "cool to be frugal" at the checkout', *Financial Times*, 12 December 2008. See

also 'Recession-hit shoppers turn to car boot sales', *Financial Times*, 16 May 2009.

25 See 'Business is booming at run-down stores', *Financial Times*, 13 April 2009. See also 'Fresh life for street markets', *Financial Times*, 14 April 2009.

26 See 'Decomposing the Retail Sales Index implied price deflator and the CPI', ONS, *Economic and Labour Market Review*, Volume Number 5, May 2008.

27 Turner, *The Credit Crunch*, pp. 21–2.

28 Source: ONS. The deflator rose 16.5 per cent y/y in April 1980, and 6.5 per cent y/y in June 1990.

29 Source: ONS.

30 See *Inflation Report*, Bank of England, August 2008.

31 Ibid., pp. 5, 8.

32 Ibid., pp. 7, 28, 35.

33 See 'Slash interest rates now or risk deepening recession, Bank of England adviser warns', *Guardian*, 21 July 2008, and 'The time for inaction is over. We have to cut rates, and cut them now', *Guardian*, 24 September 2008.

34 See BoE 'Minutes of Monetary Policy Committee Meeting', January to September 2008.

35 See 'Why the Bank of England won't cut interest rates', *The Sun*, 19 August 2008.

36 See BoE 'Minutes of the Monetary Policy Committee Meeting', 9 and 10 April 2008.

37 See Andrew Sentance, 'Monetary Policy: Sticking to the Basics', Leicester Chamber of Commerce Gala Dinner, 24 September 2008.

38 See Board of Governors of the Federal Reserve System press releases, 30 January, 18 March, 30 April, 25 June, 5 August 2008.

39 See Federal Reserve 'Minutes of the Federal Open Market Committee', 18 March 2008. See also 'Fix the credit system first', *Wall Street Journal*, 22 April 2008.

40 See Board of Governors of the Federal Reserve System press releases, 18 March, 30 April 2008.

41 See 'Another double dissent: Dallas's Fisher and Philadelphia's Plosser', *Wall Street Journal*, 30 April 2008.

42 See Board of Governors of the Federal Reserve System press release, 22 January 2008.

43 See William Poole, 'Real Estate in the US Economy', Industrial Asset Management Council Convention, St Louis, 9 October 2007.

44 Source: Thomson Reuters Datastream. The implied 3-Month Euro-Dollar Rate based on the December 2008 contract rose from 1.87

per cent on 17 March 2008 to 3.71 per cent on 16 June 2008. The implied 3-Month Euro-Sterling Rate based on the December 2008 contract climbed from 4.66 per cent on 17 March 2008 to 6.50 per cent on 19 June 2008.

45 See 'ECB chief warns interest rates may have to rise to fight inflation', AFP, 5 June 2008. See also 'ECB claims citizens support rate rise', *Financial Times*, 3 July 2008 and 'Trichet says ECB may consider raising rates in July', Bloomberg, 5 June 2008.

46 See 'Liebscher says ECB has room to raise interest rates', Bloomberg, 25 July 2008.

47 See 'Barroso backs ECB over rates', *Financial Times*, 5 July 2008.

48 Source: Eurostat. Real GDP (EA 16) fell 0.2 per cent q/q in Q2 and Q3 2008, before falling 1.6 per cent q/q in Q4. Real Domestic Demand (EA 16) slowed to 0.1 per cent q/q in Q4 2007, rose 0.5 per cent q/q in Q1 2008, dropped 0.4 per cent q/q in Q2, before rising 0.4 per cent q/q in Q3. At that point, Real Domestic Demand (EA 16) was up just 0.6 per cent y/y. It then fell 0.7 per cent q/q and 0.2 per cent y/y in Q4 2008.

49 Source: Eurostat. For Retail Sales, Deflated Turnover, Total (EA 16), the six-month change, averaged over three months, fell to –0.5 per cent in June 2008. Consumption Expenditure, Households and Non-Profit Institutions Serving Households had risen by an annualised rate of 2.0 per cent in Q3 2007, but then slowed to an annualised 0.5 per cent in Q1 2008.

50 The Dow Jones Industrials Price Index rose to 13,058.2 on 2 May 2008, and then fell to 11,422.0 on 12 September 2008, the last trading day before Lehman Brothers defaulted. The wider Wilshire 5000 Price Index fell from 14,423.8 on 16 May 2008 to 12,764.9 on 12 September 2008.

51 Source: Thomson Reuters Datastream. The gap between the UK£ 3-Month London Interbank Offered Rate and the Overnight Rate climbed from 0.51 per cent on 17 March 2008 to 0.95 per cent on 27 June 2008. The gap between the US$ 3-Month London Interbank Offered Rate and the Federal Funds (Effective) – Middle Rate rose from –0.11 per cent on 17 March 2008 to 0.96 per cent on 18 June 2008.

52 Source: BoE, Monetary and Financial Statistics, Table B2.1. Non-Residents Foreign Currency Deposits at all UK Monetary Institutions rose to £3.153 trillion at the end of March 2008 (218.4 per cent of GDP at Market Prices, based on Q1 data, annualised). Non-Residents Sterling Deposits climbed to £662.522 billion (45.9 per cent of GDP at Market Prices, based on Q1 data, annualised). The point is perhaps corroborated by the slide in sterling during 2008. It lost 24.4 per cent of its value during the year. Source: BoE: £ Broad Index – Trade Weighted.

53 See Speech by Mervyn King, Governor of the Bank of England to the CBI, Institute of Directors, Leeds Chamber of Commerce and Yorkshire Forward at the Royal Armouries, Leeds, 21 October 2008, pp. 8–9.

54 See 'Washington Mutual shares fall on concern over financial health', *Financial Times*, 25 July 2008.

55 Source: Eurostat. MFI's: Loans to Households for House Purchase peaked in March 2006, at 13.2 per cent y/y. It fell steadily thereafter, tumbling to 0.4 per cent y/y in April 2009. See also 'Fortis profit falls on further writedowns', *Financial Times*, 13 May 2008, 'Fortis shares plunge on capital-raising move', *Financial Times*, 26 June 2008, 'UBS faces more trouble with mortgage securities', *New York Times*, 10 June 2008 and 'More pain ahead for UBS?', *Wall Street Journal*, 10 June 2008.

56 While the most popular mortgage in the US is a fixed, 30-year contract, the rate is influenced by shorter-dated Treasuries. The yields for seven- to ten-year maturities have the most impact on this borrowing cost.

57 Source: Thomson Reuters Datastream. The gap between the UK£ 3-Month London Interbank Offered Rate and the Overnight Rate was still 0.72 per cent on the last trading day of August 2008. It had risen to 1.05 per cent on 11 September 2007 following the freeze in money markets over the summer of that year. This spread subsequently fell, but then rose again following the collapse of Bear Stearns to 0.88 per cent on 25 April 2008. It climbed to 0.95 per cent on 27 June 2008, edged down through July and August before accelerating higher following the collapse of Lehman Brothers. It reached a high of 2.21 per cent on 21 October 2008. The gap between the US$ 3-Month London Interbank Offered Rate and the Federal Funds (Effective) – Middle Rate had risen to a high of 0.86 per cent following the seizure of money markets over the summer of 2007. After falling back to a low of –0.23 per cent on 14 March 2008, it rose again to 0.87 per cent on the last trading day of August 2008. It then exploded to a peak of 4.03 per cent on 10 October 2008.

58 See 'South Koreans in talks over Lehman lifeline', *Financial Times*, 3 September 2008. See also 'KDB warned over Lehman stake', *Financial Times*, 8 September 2008, 'Broken brothers: How brinkmanship was not enough to save Lehman', *Financial Times*, 15 September 2008 and 'KDB, weighing Lehman investment, sees "opportunity"', Bloomberg, 22 August 2008.

59 See 'Lehman files biggest bankruptcy case as suitors balk', Bloomberg, 15 September 2008. See also 'The Lehman legacy', *Financial Times*, 13 October 2008.

60   See 'Picking over the Lehman carcass', *The Banker*, 1 December 2008. See also 'Getting Lehman wrong a second time', *Guardian*, 16 March 2009.

61   See 'This greed was beyond irresponsible', *Financial Times*, 17 September 2008 and 'What if Lehman files for bankruptcy and nothing much happens?', *Financial Times*, 15 September 2008.

62   See 'Lehman shock shakes banks, gov't', *Nikkei News*, 22 September 2008. Dollar figure based on ¥/US$ exchange rate of 104.9.

63   See 'Agency's '04 rule let banks pile up new debt', *New York Times*, 3 October 2008. See also 'SEC leverage rule change contributed to investment bank failure', www.parapundit.com/archives/005558. html, accessed 18 June 2009.

64   See 'US to take over AIG in $85 billion bailout; central banks inject cash as credit dries up', *Wall Street Journal*, 16 September 2008. See also 'Fed's $85 billion loan rescues insurer', *New York Times*, 17 September 2008.

65   See 'Statement by Secretary Henry M. Paulson, Jr. on Comprehensive Approach to Market Developments', US Department of Treasury, 19 September 2008.

66   Source: Thomson Reuters Datastream. The Dow Jones Industrials Price Index fell from 11,143.1 on 26 September 2008 to 10,365.5 on 29 September 2008.

67   See 'Government seizes WaMu and sells some assets', *New York Times*, 26 September 2008.

68   Source: Mortgage Brokers Association (MBA). In the fourth week of August 2008, the Conventional Mortgage Contract Rate, 30-Years, was 6.43 per cent, compared with 6.14 per cent in the first week of March 2008, just before Bear Stearns went bust.

69   See 'Poser for Paulson: the US Treasury chief wants a halt to public bail-outs', *Financial Times*, 12 September 2008. See also 'Winners and losers of the Fannie and Freddie bailout', *Wall Street Journal*, 7 September 2008 and 'Markets rally after Fannie and Freddie bail-out', *Financial Times*, 8 September 2008.

70   Source: MBA. The Conventional Mortgage Contract Rate, 30-Years, fell from 6.43 per cent in the fourth week of August 2008 to 5.82 per cent in the second week of September 2008. Thereafter, it climbed back up towards 6.47 per cent by the final week of October 2008. That was a fall of just 39 basis points or 0.39 per cent from the peak of 6.86 per cent recorded in the fourth week of June 2006.

71   See 'Treasury statement on financial support to the banking industry', HM Treasury, 13 October 2008. See also 'Interest rates cut to 4.5 per cent as Brown unveils £500bn bank bail-out', *Guardian*, 8 October 2008.

72 See 'High street lenders cut mortgage rates after pressure from Darling', *Financial Times*, 8 November 2008. See also 'Pass on rate cuts or risk public anger, Mandelson warns banks as HSBC chief defies Brown', *Daily Mail*, 4 November 2008.

73 For a longer analysis, see G. Tett, *Fools Gold*, Little Brown Books Group, 2009 and P. Mason, *Meltdown, The End of the Age of Greed*, Verso Books, 2009, pp. 74–80.

74 Source: BoE. Growth in M4 money supply accelerated from a low of 10.1 per cent y/y in May 2008 to 18.8 per cent y/y in February 2009.

75 Source: BoE. Lending to Other Financial Institutions accelerated to 44.7 per cent y/y in February 2009. Other Financial Institutions include leasing companies, pension funds, life insurance companies, securities dealers, investment trusts and mortgage and housing corporations. Lending to Non-Financial Corporations had slowed to 3.2 per cent y/y by February 2009, before dropping to 0.2 per cent y/y in April 2009. Furthermore, the six-month annualised rate showed a fall of 2.7 per cent in April 2009. Lending to the Personal Sector was down 5.2 per cent y/y in February 2009, before easing to −4.3 per cent y/y in April 2009.

76 See 'Peter Mandelson promises help for small businesses', *Daily Telegraph*, 23 October 2008.

77 Source: Merrill Lynch (ML): High Yield (£). The average yield on non-investment grade corporate bonds was 13.89 per cent on 12 September 2008, just before Lehman Brothers defaulted. It rose to 28.95 per cent on 11 December 2008. It carried on rising during the early months of 2009, hitting a fresh high of 34.61 per cent on 6 April.

78 Source: ML: European Issuers, High Yield (€). The average yield on non-investment grade corporate bonds was 11.58 per cent on 12 September 2008. It rose to 26.42 per cent on 8 December 2008. It fell to 21.93 per cent on 20 January 2009, rising again to 26.12 per cent on 10 March 2009, before drifting lower.

79 ML High Yield ($). The average yield on non-investment grade corporate bonds was 11.61 per cent on 12 September 2008. It rose to 22.62 per cent on 12 December 2008.

80 Source: Barclays High Yield Automotive. The average yield on non-investment grade corporate bonds for auto manufacturers rose from 15.03 per cent on 12 September 2008 to 49.91 per cent on 24 November 2008.

81 Source: Thomson Reuters Datastream, US Corporate Bond Moody's Seasoned BAA, Middle Rate. The average yield on BAA rate corporate bonds rose from 7.17 per cent on 12 September 2008 to 9.54 per cent on 31 October 2008.

82   Source: BLS. The Unemployment Rate hit a low of 4.4 per cent in
     March 2007 and rose to 6.2 per cent in September 2008. The U6
     rate, Unemployment and All Marginally Attached & Involuntary
     Part Time as a Percentage of the Labour Force, climbed from 8.0
     per cent to 11.2 per cent over the corresponding period.
83   Source: BLS. The worst month for the dotcom recession was October
     2001, when Non-Farm Employment fell 325,000. The worst month
     for the early 1990s recession was February 1991, when 306,000
     jobs were lost. The worst month for the early 1980s was May 1980,
     when 431,000 jobs disappeared.
84   Source: BLS. Non-Farm Employment shrank 741,000 in January
     2009. Private Sector Employment fell 749,000 in January 2009,
     688,000 in February, 648,000 in March and 596,000 in April.
85   Source: BLS. Workers on Involuntary Part Time, All Industries, had
     climbed from a low of 3.91 million in April 2006 to 9.08 million by
     May 2009.
86   Source: BLS.
87   Source: ONS, Labour Force Survey. Unemployed Aged 16+ rose to
     2.261 million in the three months to April 2009. The Unemployment
     Rate for Aged 16+ climbed to 7.2 per cent. Employment for Aged
     16+ fell 271,000 in the three months to April 2009, compared with
     the previous three months, the biggest fall since records began in
     1971. Total Claimant Count climbed to 1.390 million in February
     2009, an increase of 136,600 over January 2009. By May 2009, it
     had risen to 1.545 million.
88   Source: Ministerio De Economia Y Hacienda, Instituto Nacional
     De Estadistica (INE) and Eurostat. Registered Unemployment rose
     to 3.714 million (seasonally adjusted) in May 2009, compared
     with 2.129 million in December 2007. According to INE, the
     Unemployment Rate rose to 17.36 per cent in Q1 2009. According
     to Eurostat, it had climbed from 14.7 per cent in December 2008
     to 18.1 per cent by April 2009.
89   Source: Eurostat. Unemployment Rate (EA 16), seasonally
     adjusted.

Chapter 2

1   G. Turner, *The Credit Crunch*, Pluto Press, 2008, p. 149. For more
    on Japan's economic crisis from 1990 onwards, see Chapters 7
    and 8.
2   G. Turner, *Solutions to a Liquidity Trap*, GFC Economics, 2003,
    pp. 86–90, 120–1.

3   Source: Organisation for Economic Co-operation and Development (OECD), General Government Liabilities/GDP. For Japan, this ratio climbed to a peak of 175.3 per cent in 2005, and was still 170.6 per cent in 2007. That compares with a 2007 figure of 62.9 per cent in the US, 46.9 per cent in the UK, 65.5 per cent in Germany, 113.2 per cent in Italy, 70.1 per cent in France, 87.6 per cent in Belgium, 15.4 per cent in Australia and 64.1 per cent in Canada.

4   Turner, *The Credit Crunch*, pp. 148–58.

5   Source: S&P/Case-Shiller, Home Price Index. This showed house prices easing during the final months of 2005. The m/m rate peaked on the 10-City composite index in March and April 2005, at 1.7 per cent (non-seasonally adjusted). It dropped to 0.5 per cent by December 2005 and 0.2 per cent in January 2006. It eventually went negative in July 2006, dropping 0.1 per cent, and was still falling in March 2009, when it declined 2.1 per cent.

    However, data from the National Association of Realtors showed prices falling sooner. Using seasonally adjusted data for the Median Price of Existing One-Family Houses Sold during the month shows that the m/m change fell from 2.5 per cent in June 2005 to –1.2 per cent in November 2005, and –1.9 per cent in December 2005. The six-month change, again based on seasonally adjusted data, fell from 9.1 per cent in August 2005 to 2.0 per cent in December 2005, and went negative in March 2006. With the exception of December 2006 and two months in 2007, it was still falling in April 2009. It is a similar story for the Average Price of Existing One-Family Houses Sold during the month with the m/m rate turning negative in November 2005, and the six-month rate going negative in March 2006.

    For new home sales, the Median Price of New One-Family Houses Sold during the month fell in October and November 2005 based on the seasonally adjusted m/m change. The six-month rate went negative in March 2006, although this decline was initially rather more erratic. For Average Price of New One-Family Houses Sold during the month, the first m/m decline was in October 2005, and the six-month rate went negative in March 2006.

    The National Association of Home Builders Housing Market Index peaked at 72.0 in June 2005, fell to 57.0 in December 2005 and carried on falling in 2006, 2007 and 2008, hitting a low of 8.0 in January 2009.

6   Source: S&P/Case-Shiller, Home Price Index, 10-City Composite, December 2008. Using the 10-City Composite Index, house prices dropped 19.2 per cent y/y. Using the 20-City Composite Index, house prices were falling 18.6 per cent y/y.

7   See '"Green" plan aims to consign Argentina's debt woes to history', *Financial Times*, 18 March 2009.

8   Source: Federal Reserve, Flow of Funds (FoF), Table L.107 Rest of the World. At the end of Q4 2008, overseas investors held $3,187.4 billion of US Treasury Securities. Official investors held $2,125.1 billion, while private investors held $1,062.2 billion.

9   Source: Federal Reserve. C&I (Commercial and Industrial) Loan Survey – Large and Medium Firms, Banks Tightening Credit. The percentage (net) balance for Q4 2008 rose to 83.6. This shows the net number of respondents that have experienced banks tightening credit. In this respect, Figures 2.1 and 2.2 may not show the full extent of the correlation, because this net balance does not indicate by how much each bank is tightening credit or raising margins.

10 M. Friedman & A.J. Schwartz, *A Monetary History of the United States, 1867–1960*, Princeton University Press, 1963, p. 355. 'The impairment in the market value of assets held by banks, particularly in their bond portfolios, was the most important source of impairment of capital leading to bank suspensions, rather than the default of specific loans or of specific bond issues.'

11 Ibid., p. 390.

12 Ibid., pp. 304, 323. See also www.economagic.com/em-cgi/data.exe/fedstl/baa+2 (accessed 1 June 2009), which puts the high for BAA yields as 11.0 per cent, in May 1932, and the low-point for the year as 7.6 per cent.

13 Ibid., p. 323.

14 Source: Federal Reserve, FoF, Table L.107 Rest of the World. At the end of Q4 2007, private investors overseas held $615.3 billion of Agency- and GSE-backed securities. Within a year, this had fallen to $395.6 billion. Official overseas holdings (largely central banks) of Agency- and GSE-backed securities were $956.4 billion at the end of Q4 2007, and only fell to $935.5 billion a year later.

15 See 'Bear Stearns tells fund investors "no value left"', Bloomberg, 18 July 2007. See also 'Buyers avoid Bear Stearns' cut-priced sale', *Financial Times*, 3 July 2007.

16 Source: Markit. www.markit.com/en/products/data/indices/structured-finance-indices/abx/abx-prices.page?, accessed 6 May 2009.

17 Friedman & Schwartz, *A Monetary History of the United States*, p. 324.

18 Ibid., p. 326.

19 Ibid., p. 326.

20 Ibid., p. 330.

21 See 'Fair value: the pragmatic solution', CNNMoney.com, 21
    November 2008. www.money.cnn.com/2008/11/21/news/fair.value.
    compromise.fortune/index.htm, accessed 6 May 2009.
22 See 'Congress helped banks defang key rule', *Wall Street Journal*,
    3 June 2009. See also 'Putting a price on toxic assets could cost
    public finances', *Financial Times*, 26 March 2009.
23 Friedman & Schwartz, *A Monetary History of the United States*,
    p. 330.
24 Ibid., p. 368. The Open Market Policy Conference (OMPC) was
    established in March 1930 and replaced the Open Market Investment
    Committee. The latter had consisted of the five governors of the New
    York, Boston, Chicago, Cleveland and Philadelphia Reserve Banks.
    The OMPC consisted of all twelve bank governors.
25 Ibid., p. 339.
26 Ibid., p. 341.
27 Ibid., p. 370.
28 Ibid., p. 370.
29 Ibid., p. 371.
30 Ibid., p. 372.
31 Ibid., p. 372.
32 Ibid., p. 372.
33 Ibid., pp. 372, 373.
34 See Ben Bernanke's speech, 'The Crisis and the Policy Response',
    The Stamp Lecture, London School of Economics, 13 January 2009,
    pp. 6–7.
35 See Friedman & Schwartz, *A Monetary History of the United States*,
    p. 374.
36 Ibid., p. 374.
37 The Bank of United States failed on 11 December 1930. At that
    point, it had been the largest banking collapse during the Great
    Depression. See Friedman & Schwartz, *A Monetary History of the
    United States*, pp. 309, 310.
38 Ibid., p. 377.
39 Ibid., p. 378.
40 Ibid., p. 378, 379.
41 Ibid., p. 379. This conference was the first meeting at which there
    was explicit reference to the issue of free gold. The problem of free
    gold was later cited as a major reason for the Federal Reserve's failure
    to pursue more aggressive open market purchases. However, this
    argument has since been rejected by a number of economists. See
    Friedman & Schwartz, *A Monetary History of the United States*,
    pp. 399–406.
42 Ibid., p. 380.

43 Ibid., p. 384.
44 Ibid., p. 384.
45 Ibid., p. 385.
46 Ibid., p. 385.
47 Ibid., p. 386.
48 Ibid., p. 386.
49 Ibid., p. 386.
50 Ibid., p. 387.
51 Ibid., p. 386.
52 Ibid., pp. 386, 387.
53 Ibid., p. 389. The OMPC 'recommended purchases not to exceed $15m a week – except in unusual or unforeseen circumstances – but not less than $5m a week for the next four weeks'.
54 Ibid., p. 389.
55 Ibid., p. 390. Holdings of government securities were reduced by $90 million in January, despite the concern of US Treasury officials.
56 Ibid., p. 391.
57 Ibid., p. 421. This was done under the 'wartime measure of 6 October 1917, which conferred broad powers over banking and currency upon the President of the United States'.
58 Ibid., pp. 422–5.
59 Ibid., pp. 427–8.
60 The Savings and Loan crisis of the 1980s and 1990s is commonly referred to as the S&L crisis. It saw the failure of 745 savings and loan associations (S&Ls or thrifts). An S&L association is a financial institution in the US that accepts savings deposits and makes mortgage loans. The ultimate cost of the crisis was $160.1 billion, of which $124.6 billion was paid directly by the US government.
61 Turner, *The Credit Crunch*, pp. 190–1.
62 Friedman & Schwartz, *A Monetary History of the United States*, p. 518.
63 A.M. Meulendyke, *US Monetary Policy & Financial Markets*, Federal Reserve Bank of New York, 1998, p. 22. The Federal Reserve Total Holdings (of assets, including Government debt or securities) still rose 37.1 per cent from the year before.
64 Ibid., p. 22. Federal Reserve Total Holdings fell 4.4 per cent in 1934 from 1933 to $2,430.4 billion. But Holdings of Treasury Certificates fell from $425.1 billion to $0.0 billion. Holdings of Treasury Notes went up from $1,053.2 billion to $1,507.1 billion.
65 G. Tily, *Keynes's General Theory, the Rate of Interest and 'Keynesian' Economics*, Palgrave Macmillan, 2007, p. 69.
66 The letter was written by Walter Lippmann, a 'celebrated' journalist and broadcaster for the National Broadcasting Company of America.

67 Tily, *Keynes's General Theory*, p. 69.

68 See *Historical Statistics of the United States, Colonial Times to 1970, Part 2*, US Department of Commerce, Bureau of the Census, 1975, p. 667. The Index for US Industrial Production fell from 23 in 1929 to 12 in 1932, before rising to 14 in 1933. A less pessimistic assessment comes from the National Bureau of Economic Research, which shows that Manufacturing Output in Volume Terms fell 17.9 per cent between 1929 and 1932, before rising to a level in 1937 that was 17.9 per cent above the previous cyclical peak, of 1929.

See also, Federal Reserve, St Louis. The monthly data shows a bigger recovery from July 1932. The monthly Seasonally Adjusted Index for US Industrial Production (2002=100) rose from a low of 4.1179 in July 1932 to a high of 6.6728 a year later, a gain of 62.0 per cent.

The Seasonally Adjusted Index for US Industrial Production (2002=100) peaked in July 1929 at 8.8670 and finally climbed back to 9.0173 in December 1936.

69 See *Historical Statistics of the United States, Colonial Times to 1970, Part 1*, US Department of Commerce, Bureau of the Census, 1975, p. 224.

70 Source: Federal Reserve, St Louis. The Seasonally Adjusted Index for US Industrial Production (2002=100) fell to 4.1179 in July 1932, before recovering to 4.6589 in October and November 1932. It then fell again, to 4.2381 in March 1933, before rising swiftly to a high of 6.6728 for the year in July 1933. The July 1932 low was 2.8 per cent below the March 1933 trough.

71 See *Historical Statistics of the United States, Colonial Times to 1970, Part 1*, p. 224.

72 Friedman & Schwartz, *A Monetary History of the United States*, p. 520. 'The 1936–37 increases in reserve requirements apparently had their origin in proposals made by the New York Bank. Beginning in early 1934, the Bank staff prepared a series of internal memoranda, some circulated also to the Federal Open Market Committee, in which it examined the problem of excess reserves, emphasized the potential dangers they raised, and considered alternative ways to control them.'

73 Ibid., p. 458. When 'the rise in reserves requirements immobilized the accumulated cash, they proceeded rather promptly to accumulate additional cash for liquidity purposes'. For more, see also pp. 526–8.

74 See *Historical Statistics of the United States, Colonial Times to 1970, Part 1*, p. 126.

75 Ibid., p. 224. Gross National Product at 1958 prices fell 5.1 per cent between 1937 and 1938.

76 See Friedman & Schwartz, *A Monetary History of the United States*, pp. 493–5. Wage rises were initially promoted through the codes established under the National Industrial Recovery Act, passed on 16 June 1933. The codes were declared unconstitutional in 1935, but they still had some interim impact. Thereafter, wages were supported by the National Labour Relations Act and the enactment of minimum wage laws. Labour costs were also raised by laws introducing a range of new taxes, including social security taxes, from 1935. For more, see K. Rose, *The Economics of Recession and Revival*, Yale University Press, 1954, and A.J. Badger, *FDR: The First Hundred Days*, Hill and Wang, 2007.

77 Friedman & Schwartz, *A Monetary History of the United States*, p. 526. 'The increase in reserve requirements did have important current effects... the timing of the behaviour of the money stock documents this conclusion in detail.'

78 See *Historical Statistics of the United States, Colonial Times to 1970, Part 1*, p. 126.

79 Ibid., p. 126.

80 Friedman & Schwartz, *A Monetary History of the United States*, p. 557. See also Note 2 in Chapter 8.

81 Ibid., p. 561.

82 Meulendyke, *US Monetary Policy & Financial Markets*, p. 22.

83 Tily, *Keynes's General Theory*, p. 51. On 28 April 1925, Winston Churchill, as Chancellor, took Britain back on a full internal gold standard at the historic rate of £3 17s 10½d per ounce.

84 See 'The slump of the 1930s and the crisis today', Chris Harman, *International Socialism*, Winter 2009, Number 121, p. 31.

85 See 'Unemployment statistics from 1881 to the present day', Labour Market Trends, January 1996. The unemployment rate rose from 10.9 per cent in April 1925 to 14.6 per cent in June 1926.

86 Tily, *Keynes's General Theory*, p. 59.

87 Ibid., p. 60.

88 Ibid., p. 60.

89 Ibid., p. 60.

90 Ibid., p. 61.

91 See 'The Working-Class Owner-Occupied House of the 1930s', Alan Crisp, M.Litt Oxford thesis, 1998. See Introduction, p. 3. See also S. Howson & D. Winch, *The Economic Advisory Council 1930–1939: A Study in Economic Advice during Depression and Recovery*, Cambridge University Press, 1977, p. 111.

92 Source: Financial Services Authority. After the credit crunch hit the UK in August 2007, nine building societies, or former building societies, were taken over by other financial institutions or rescued by the government. These were Northern Rock, Bradford & Bingley, Halifax (subsequently part of HBOS), Alliance & Leicester, Dunfermline, Derbyshire, Cheshire, Barnsley, and Scarborough.

Chapter 3

1 M. Friedman & A.J. Schwartz, *A Monetary History of the United States, 1867–1960*, Princeton University Press, 1963, pp. 395–6, 399–406.

2 G. Turner, *The Credit Crunch*, Pluto Press, 2008, pp. 109–34.

3 See *Solutions to a Liquidity Trap*, GFC Economics, 2003, pp. 145–68.

4 See *Could Monetary Policy Have Prevented Deep Recession?*, available from www.gfceconomics.com.

5 See 'Treasuries rise as traders prepare for tomorrow's Fed purchases', Bloomberg, 26 March 2009. In a small number of cases interest rates have indeed turned negative. One-month US Treasury Bill Rates, for example, went negative on 26 December 2008, when they reached –0.05 per cent and again on 25 March 2009, when they fell to –0.0152 per cent.

6 See 'Fed study puts ideal interest rate at –5%', *Financial Times*, 27 April 2009.

7 The question of how much quantitative easing contributed to Japan's economic recovery is open to debate. The whole point of quantitative easing is to drive and keep bond yields low. Quantitative easing was not introduced until 19 March 2001. By that point, 10-year Japanese government bond yields had already fallen from a high of 7.92 per cent on 26 September 1990 to 1.13 per cent on 18 March 2001. However, yields did eventually fall further in the second half of 2002, and hit a low of 0.43 per cent on 12 June 2003. The stock market finally reached a low on 28 April 2003, when the Nikkei 225 fell to 7,607.9. It recovered soon after, helped in part by the nationalisation of Resona Bank on 17 May 2003.

Other factors contributed to the stock market and economic recovery, including a reflation of the US housing market and China's boom. But the policy may have succeeded, by at least holding bond yields down even as the recovery upswing gathered momentum. Indeed, Japanese government bond yields remained very low throughout the recovery. During the 1990s, many of Japan's economic recoveries were short-circuited by a premature rise in borrowing costs, led by rising bond yields. That did not happen in the 2003 recovery, although the upswing was cut short by the collapse of the US housing market and the global credit crunch. See Turner, *Solutions to a Liquidity Trap*, pp. 169–74.

8   See 'U.S. office vacancies hit 15.2% – and rising', *Wall Street Journal*, 3 April 2009. See also 'Commercial property faces crisis', *Wall Street Journal*, 26 March 2009.

9   I. Fisher, *Booms and Depressions*, Adelphi Company, 1932, pp. 8–27. See also Turner, *The Credit Crunch*, pp. 153–5, 157, 187.

10   Source: Federal Reserve, Factors Affecting Reserve Balances. In the first week of March 2008, US Treasury Securities Held by the Fed were $713.365 billion. By the first week of July 2008, this had fallen to $478.838 billion, a drop of 32.9 per cent.

11   Source: Mortgage Bankers Association of America (MBA). Residential Mortgage Loans: All Foreclosures Started rose to 1.19 per cent of all borrowers in Q2, 1.09 per cent in Q3 and 1.01 per cent in Q4 2008. That compares with 0.35 per cent in Q4 1991 at the worst point of the previous housing downturn. Residential Mortgage Loans: All Foreclosure Inventory rose to 2.97 per cent of all borrowers in Q3 2008 and 3.30 per cent in Q4 2008, compared with a peak of 1.04 per cent in Q4 1991 and Q1, Q2 and Q3 1992. Residential Mortgage Loans: All, Total Delinquent rose to 6.99 per cent of all borrowers in Q3 2008 and 7.88 per cent in Q4 2008. Combining foreclosure inventory and delinquency implies that 9.96 per cent of all homeowners with a mortgage were in arrears or in some stage of foreclosure by the end of Q3 2008. That climbed to 11.18 per cent by the end of Q4 2008 and 12.97 per cent by the end of Q1 2009.

12   Source: Federal Reserve, Factors Affecting Reserve Balances. Total assets held by the Federal Reserve were $908.991 billion in the first week of September 2008. By the first week of November 2008 that had risen to $1,970.680 billion.

13   The share price peaked on 29 December 2006 at $55.70 and fell to $5.95 on 24 November 2008. www.citigroup.com/cit/fin/index.htm, accessed 5 May 2009.

14   See 'Citigroup gets guarantee on $306 billion of assets', Bloomberg, 24 November 2008.

15   See Board of Governors of the Federal Reserve System press release, 25 November 2008. The first mention of 'credit easing' came from the Federal Reserve Chairman on 13 January 2009. Ben Bernanke, 'The Crisis and the Policy Response', The Stamp Lecture, London School of Economics, 13 January 2009, p. 5.

16   Source: US Federal Reserve, FoF, L. 210, Agency- and GSE-backed Securities. By the end of Q4 2008, there were $4,965.1 billion

Agency- and GSE-backed mortgage pools outstanding. Liabilities of Government-sponsored enterprises were \$3,224.1 billion.

17 Source: S&P/Case-Shiller, Home Price Index, 10-City Composite, November 2008.

18 Source: Federal Reserve (FoF), Financial Liabilities – Households & Nonprofits, and Bureau of Labor Statistics (BLS), Disposable Personal Income. The ratio of financial liabilities to disposable income rose from 79.2 per cent in Q1 1988 to 138.4 per cent in Q1 2008.

19 Source: Merrill Lynch High Yield Cash Pay (\$). The average yield rose from 11.54 per cent on 1 September 2008 to a high of 22.62 per cent on 12 December 2008.

20 See Board of Governors of the Federal Reserve System press release, 16 December 2008.

21 See Turner, *The Credit Crunch*, pp. 175–80.

22 Even though the Bank of England was the first major central bank to commit to quantitative easing in 2009, it still failed to understand how the policy would work. See letter from Mervyn King, Governor of the Bank of England (BoE), to the Chancellor of Exchequer, Alistair Darling, 17 February 2009, p. 2. The Bank of England Governor argued that purchases of assets financed through central bank money 'would provide scope for the monetary base to be expanded. This would act to boost the broad supply of money and credit and increase the liquidity of private sector portfolios, thereby raising nominal spending.' See also 'Minutes of the Monetary Policy Committee, 4 and 5 March 2009', BoE, 18 March 2009, p. 8. 'Under the operations now under consideration, the Committee would instead be focussing more directly on the quantity of money it supplied in exchange for assets held by the private sector. By increasing the supply of money in the economy, these operations would cause nominal spending to rise.'

23 See 'Bond yields can offer a solution to global woes', Michael Mackenzie, *Financial Times*, 29 November 2008. 'The 10-year notes are the benchmark and safest of safe-haven assets.'

24 See for example, J.M. Keynes, *The General Theory of Employment, Interest and Money*, Macmillan Cambridge University Press, 1973, p. 235. 'The money-rate of interest, by setting the pace for all other commodity rates of interest, holds back production of these other commodities without being capable of stimulating investment for the production of money, which by hypothesis cannot be produced.'

25 G. Tily, *Keynes's General Theory, the Rate of Interest and 'Keynesian' Economics*, Palgrave Macmillan, 2007, p. 84 and Keynes, *The General Theory of Employment, Interest and Money*, p. 203.

26 Source: Thomson Reuters Datastream. The Federal Funds target fell from a high of 9.81 per cent in June 1989 to 3.0 per cent in September 1992. The 10-year Treasury yield dropped from a high of 9.55 per cent on 20 March 1989 to 5.17 per cent on 15 October 1993. Source: MBA. The Conventional Mortgage, Contract Rate, 30-Years, dropped from 10.56 per cent on 27 April 1990 to 6.59 per cent on 15 October 1993.

27 Keynes, *The General Theory of Employment, Interest and Money*, p. 202. See also Turner, *The Credit Crunch*, p. 164.

28 See 'European states struggle to raise money', *Financial Times*, 22 October 2008, 'German bond auction bodes ill', *Financial Times*, 8 January 2009, 'Debt fears prompt UK gilt auction failure', *Financial Times*, 26 March 2009, 'Bond concerns overshadow encouraging data', *Financial Times*, 26 March 2009, 'Treasury sale trips up stocks', *Wall Street Journal*, 11 June 2009, 'U.K. employs banks to market bonds', *Wall Street Journal*, 17 June 2009 and 'Gilt syndication arrives', *Wall Street Journal*, 17 June 2009.

29 Source: Bank of Japan and Thomson Reuters Datastream. The differential between the Bank of Japan's discount rate and the 10-year JGB yield rose from a low of 0.4 per cent in January 1991 to a high of 2.93 per cent in August 1994. See also Turner, *The Credit Crunch*, pp.162, 163, 166. See also Turner, *Solutions to a Liquidity Trap*, pp. 172–4.

30 See 'Sliding bond yields spur bubble talk', *Financial Times*, 2 December 2008.

31 Counter cyclical capital ratios were a tool that drew increasing scrutiny. Sir Andrew Large, former deputy governor of the Bank of England, argued for their introduction. See 'Central banks must be the debt watchdogs', *Financial Times*, 5 January 2009. Lord Turner, chair of the UK's Financial Services Authority, also began to discuss the merits of counter cyclical capital rules. See 'Adair Turner interview transcript', *Financial Times*, 10 December 2008. See also 'Banker echoes call to review capital ratios', *Financial Times*, 26 March 2009.

32 Tily, *Keynes's General Theory, the Rate of Interest and 'Keynesian' Economics*, pp. 78–9.

33 See 'Charlie Bean Interview', *Financial Times*, 17 December 2008.

34 Source: BLS. Crude Materials, For Further Processing, fell 18.5 per cent y/y in November 2008. By May 2009, they were falling 41.3 per cent y/y. Crude Non-Food Materials Less Energy, For Further Processing, dropped 22.4 per cent y/y in November 2008. By May 2009, they were falling 36.7 per cent y/y.

35 Source: Department of Commerce-Bureau of Census and Bureau of Economic Analysis (BEA). Total Retail Sales And Food Services sales fell by a 3-month/3-month annualised rate of 22.6 per cent in December 2008. New Passenger Car Sales dropped 33.0 per cent y/y, and New Passenger Light Truck Sales were down 38.1 per cent y/y in December 2008.

36 Source: Institute for Supply Management (ISM), Purchasing Managers Index (Manufacturing Survey). The Manufacturing ISM Index fell from 49.3 in August 2008 to 32.9 in December 2008, its lowest level since June 1980.

37 Source: Thomson Reuters Datastream, US Corporate Bond Moody's Seasoned BAA, Middle Rate. The average yield on BAA rate corporate bonds peaked at 9.54 per cent on 31 October 2008 and two days after the Fed's meeting on 15–16 December, BAA yields had dipped to 8.11 per cent. Significantly, non-investment corporate bond yields, which closely tracked unemployment, began to fall more quickly too. The Merrill Lynch High Yield ($) fell from a peak of 22.62 per cent on 12 December 2008 to 17.72 per cent on 10 February 2009. The Conventional Mortgage Contract Rate, 30-Years, fell from 5.99 per cent in the third week of November 2008 to 5.03 per cent in the last week of December 2008.

38 Ben Bernanke, 'The Crisis and the Policy Response', The Stamp Lecture, London School of Economics, 13 January 2009.

39 Source: National Association of Realtors. Months Supply of One-Family & Condominium Homes on the Market was still 10.2 in the final three months of 2008, compared with a low of 3.6 in January 2005.

40 Source: Thomson Reuters Datastream. The Dow Jones Industrials fell from 8,474.0 on 12 January 2009 to 6,547.1 on 9 March 2009, a fall of 22.7 per cent.

41 See US Department of the Treasury press release 'Treasury Department releases details on Public Private Partnership Investment Program', 23 March 2009.

42 See Federal Deposit Insurance Corporation Public-Private Investment Program White Paper, pp. 1, 2, www.fdic.gov/llp/PPIPWhitePaper.pdf, accessed 23 March 2009. 'This program should facilitate price discovery and should help, over time, to reduce the excessive liquidity discounts embedded in current legacy asset prices.'

43 See Bank of England News Release, 5 March 2009. The Bank of England announced that it would 'undertake a programme of asset purchases of £75 billion financed by the issuance of central bank reserves'. This was later increased to £125 billion on 7 May 2009.

44   See Board of Governors of the Federal Reserve System press release, 18 March 2009.
45   See Monthly Treasury Statement, April 2009. The Federal deficit for the first eight months of Fiscal Year 2009 was $802.3 billion compared with $454.8 billion in Fiscal Year 2008. The Budget Estimate for the Full Fiscal Year (2009) was, at this stage, $1,752.1 billion. That was then revised higher to $1.80 trillion by the Congressional Budget Office. That was equivalent to 12.8 per cent of GDP, based on Q1 2009 data (source: BEA).
46   Source: Thomson Reuters Datastream. The US Treasury 10-year yield rose rapidly from a low of 2.08 per cent on 18 December 2008. It broke above 3.0 per cent on 28 April 2009 and hit 3.93 per cent on 10 June 2009.
47   Source: RealtyTrac. See www.realtytrac.com/ContentManagement/PressRelease.aspx, accessed 22 June 2009. The figures for each month do not include multiple filings. But one household may receive more than one filing over several months, ranging from notice of default (the first stage of foreclosure) through to bank repossessions (the final stage of foreclosure).
48   See 'Banks ramp up foreclosures', *Wall Street Journal*, 15 April 2009 and 'Firms to get up to $9.9 billion to modify mortgages', *Wall Street Journal*, 16 April 2009.
49   See www.whitehouse.gov/blog/09/02/18/9-million-plus/, accessed 22 June 2009.
50   See Making Home Affordable, Summary of Guidelines, US Department of the Treasury, Press Release 4 March 2009.
51   See 'More prime foreclosures; more re-defaults', www.globaleconomicanalysis.blogspot.com/2009/05/more-prime-foreclosures-more-re-html, accessed 2 June 2009. 'The problem is not on that "front-end" ratio, but on the back end, which is all of the borrowers other debt (credit cards, car loans, student loans, etc.).... other debt is so high that most of today's troubled borrowers cannot afford any loan payment at all even at a very modest debt-to-income ratio.'
52   Source: MBA, Residential Mortgage Loans, All Foreclosures Started. See also Federal National Mortgage Association, Form 10-Q, for the quarterly period ended 31 March 2009, p. 155. The lender initiated moratoria for the periods 26 November 2008 through 31 January 2009 and 17 February 2009 through 6 March 2009.
53   Source: MBA, Residential Mortgage Loans, All Foreclosure Inventory.
54   Source: MBA, Residential Mortgage Loans, All Total Delinquent.

55 Source: MBA, Residential Mortgage Loans, All 90+ Days Delinquent.

56 Source: Federal National Mortgage Association, Form 10-Q, for the quarterly period ended 31 March 2009, pp. 47, 155.

57 See 'Lenders Voluntarily Delaying Majority of Scheduled Foreclosures', The Truth About Mortgage.com, 17 June 2009.

58 See 'RealtyTrac: More Than 700,000 Bank Owned Properties in Database', The Truth About Mortgage.com, 13 June 2009. RealtyTrac reported that it had 700,000 properties on its database alone, that had been repossessed by banks, but were not on the market.

59 Source: MBA. Residential Mortgage Loans, Sub-Prime, Total Delinquent and Prime, Total Delinquent. The proportion of sub-prime borrowers that were delinquent had risen from 20.03 per cent in Q3 2008 to 24.95 per cent in Q1 2009. The proportion of prime borrowers that were delinquent had climbed from 4.34 per cent to 6.06 per cent over the corresponding period.

60 Source: MBA, Residential Mortgage Loans, All Total Delinquent plus All Foreclosure Inventory.

61 Ben Bernanke, *Essays on the Great Depression*, Princeton University Press, 2000, pp. 77, 153.

62 Ibid., p. viii.

63 Ibid., p. 6.

64 Ibid., pp. 66–7.

65 See Ben Bernanke, *Japanese Monetary Policy: A Case of Self-Induced Paralysis?* Princeton University, 1999.

Chapter 4

1 See *Historical Statistics of the United States, Colonial Times to 1970, Part 1*, US Department of Commerce, Bureau of the Census, 1975, p. 126. See also 'Unemployment statistics from 1881 to the present day', Labour Market Trends, January 1996.

2 The UK economy was supported by an increase in government spending, which rose by a real 19.5 per cent y/y in 1938. Source: C.H. Feinstein, *National Income, Expenditure & Output of the UK 1855–1965*, Cambridge University Press, 1972, p. 15.

3 J.M. Keynes, *The Economic Consequences of the Peace*, Labour Research Department, 1920.

4 For more on the German banking crises, see C.P. Kindleberger, *The World in Depression*, University of California Press, 1986, pp. 133–4, 143, 148–53, 295.

5 Ibid., pp. 163–4. Former Japanese Prime Minister Korekiyo Takahashi, a leading advocate of the Keynes prescription, was assassinated in 1936, paving the way for militarists to increase defence spending more quickly.

6 Ibid., pp. 237–8.

7 See 'Obama sets expansive goal for jobs', *Washington Post*, 23 November 2008, and 'Obama expands goals of stimulus', *Financial Times*, 22 December 2008. See also 'Conference Report on American Recovery and Reinvestment Act', 11 February 2009, www.online. wsj.com/public/resources/documents/recoveryactfactsheet021209. doc, accessed 18 May 2009.

8 Source: Deutsche Bundesbank, Negotiated Wage And Salary Level, Overall Economy – On Hourly Basis, and Statistisches Bundesamt, Consumer Price Index. Between 1999 and 2008, hourly wages rose by an average 1.8 per cent y/y. Adjusted for the Consumer Price Index, hourly wages rose by 0.2 per cent y/y over the period. Source: Ministry of Health, Labour and Welfare, Japan, Average Monthly Cash Earnings – All Industries, and Statistics Bureau of MIC, CPI, National Measure. Monthly Cash Earnings fell by an average of 0.9 per cent y/y. Adjusted by the Consumer Price Index they fell by an average of 0.7 per cent y/y.

9 Source: Bureau of Labor Statistics (BLS) and Office for National Statistics. In the US, the Constant (1982) Dollar Adjusted, Median Usual Weekly Earnings, Employed Full Time, Wage and Salary Workers, was $323 in 2008, the same as in 2000. In the UK, the Median Gross Weekly Pay for All Employees rose from £299.6 in 2000 to £388.4 in 2008. Adjusted by the Consumer Price Index, Harmonised European Union Basis, this was a real gain of 13.0, or an annualised rise of 1.5 per cent. Adjusted by the Retail Price Index, it was an increase of 3.4 per cent, an annualised gain of 0.4 per cent.

10 Kindelberger, *The World in Depression*, pp. 61–5.

11 See 'Free trade is the gateway to recovery', Peter Mandelson, *The Times*, 16 March 2009, and 'Mandelson warns on protectionism', BBC News, 31 January 2009. www.news.bbc.co.uk/1/hi/uk/7863047. stm, accessed 5 June 2009.

12 See 'Gordon Brown urges EU not to retreat into protectionism', *Guardian*, 24 March 2009.

13 G. Turner, *The Credit Crunch*, Pluto Press, 2008, pp. ix–x.

14 See 'Squaring up to Burberry', *Observer*, 25 March 2007.

15 See '"Axe queen" behind closure of Burberry plant', *Western Mail*, 11 December 2006.

16 See Graph: Performance for Burberry Group from *Financial Times*'s Market Data.

17 See 'Hoover cuts 300 jobs with Welsh plant closure', *Daily Telegraph*, 7 March 2009. See also 'Hoover to close in a week', *South Wales Echo*, 7 March 2009.

18 See 'Hotpoint: End of a proud manufacturing history as Indesit pulls the plug on production line', *Peterborough Evening Telegraph*, 16 April 2009.

19 See 'Stagecoach warns of job cuts in spite of rise in passenger numbers', *Guardian*, 4 December 2008.

20 See 'Financial Times warns of 60 job losses', *Daily Telegraph*, 22 October 2008.

21 See 'Burberry to cut up to 290 UK jobs', BBC News, 20 January 2009. www.news.bbc.co.uk/1/hi/business/7839200.stm, accessed 18 May 2009. See also, 'Burberry plans job cuts in Castleford and axes Yorkshire factory', *Yorkshire Evening Post*, 17 April 2009.

22 See 'Bargain-hungry tourists boost Burberry', *Financial Times*, 21 April 2008.

23 See 'T-Mobile move threatens 500 jobs', BBC News, 9 April 2009. www.news.bbc.co.uk/1/hi/scotland/tayside_and_central/7991496.stm, accessed 9 June 2009. See also 'BT cuts contractors' pay by up to 30 per cent amid growing wage squeeze', *Guardian*, 10 April 2009.

24 See 'Logica benefits from clients' cost cutting', *Financial Times*, 25 February 2009.

25 See 'Election results: Tories celebrate winning in Wales after Labour's "night of shame"', *Guardian*, 8 June 2009. The Labour Party's share of the vote in Wales fell 12.2 percentage points compared with a year earlier. See also 'Disaster for Labour helps BNP to claim Euro victory in Yorkshire', *Yorkshire Post*, 8 June 2009.

26 See 'North American job cuts at IBM', *Financial Times*, 26 March 2009 and 'Tech companies help clients win stimulus funds', *Sacramento Business Journal*, 7 April 2009.

27 See 'Getting to $787 billion', *Wall Street Journal*, 17 February 2009. See also 'Conference Report on American Recovery and Reinvestment Act', 11 February 2009.

28 See 'Tomorrow's scapegoats', *Financial Times*, 25 June 2008 and 'Pressure builds for Whitehall efficiency savings', *Financial Times*, 21 April 2009.

29 Source: General Administration of Customs, China. The Trade Balance for Machinery and Electronic Equipment reached $205.0 billion in 2008, up from $85.6 billion in 2006, a rise of 139.4 per cent. The Trade Balance for Textile Manufactures climbed from

$112.4 billion to $154.3 billion over the same period, a rise of 37.3 per cent.

30 Source: Economist Intelligence Unit (EIU) and General Statistics Office. GDP per capita in China was $3,160.0 in 2008, but in Vietnam it was $1,010.0. Textile exports from Vietnam rose 35.2 per cent y/y in 2007 and 17.6 per cent y/y in 2008. Between 2000 and 2008, they climbed by 404.6 per cent.

31 Source: General Administration of Customs, People's Republic of China. Exports fell by an average of 20.1 per cent y/y between January and March 2009.

32 See 'Domestic impact: unemployment poses a new challenge to the Party', *Financial Times*, 1 April 2009.

33 Source: BLS. The Consumer Price Index All Items Less Food & Energy peaked during the S&L crisis at 5.7 per cent y/y in February 1991. The peak during the next housing crisis was 2.9 per cent y/y in September 2006. The Consumer Price Index, All Items, All Urban Sample, peaked during the S&L crisis at 6.3 per cent y/y in October 1990, and then at 5.6 per cent y/y in July 2008, reflecting the run-up in food and energy prices. It soon fell to –0.7 per cent y/y by April 2009.

Chapter 5

1 For more, see J. Choonara, *Unravelling Capitalism: A Guide to Marxist Political Economy*, Bookmarks Publications, 2009.

2 K. Marx, *Grundrisse*, 1973, pp. 749, 750. See also Choonara, *Unravelling Capitalism*, pp. 74–8.

3 See K. Marx, *Capital*, II, 2, p. 20. 'It is sheer tautology to say that crises are caused by the scarcity of effective consumption, or of effective consumers... if one were to attempt to give this tautology the semblance of a profounder justification by saying that the working-class receives too small a portion of its own product and the evil would be remedied as soon as it receives a larger share of it and its wages increase in consequence, one could only remark that crises are always prepared by precisely a period in which wages rise generally and the working-class actually gets a larger share of that part of the annual product which is intended for consumption. From the point of view of these advocates of sound and "simple" (!) common sense, such a period should rather remove the crisis.'

4 Source: Merrill Lynch. The spread between High Yield ($) Corporate Bond and 10-year Treasuries fell to a low of 2.66 per cent on 12 June 2007. That compares with a low of 2.59 per cent recorded on 25 August 1997.

5 Ben Bernanke, 'The Global Savings Glut and the US Current Account Deficit', The Sandridge Lecture, Virginia Association of Economics, 10 March 2005.

6 See K. Marx, *Capital*, Volume 3, p. 485.

7 Source: US Department of Commerce. The Business Inventories/Sales Ratio fell from a high of 1.56 in January 1992 to a low of 1.24 in January 2006, before the credit crisis triggered a rise to 1.46 in December 2008 and January 2009.

8 In the UK, the minimum wage was raised to £5.73 per hour for adults aged 22 and over on 1 October 2008. In the US, the federal minimum wage for covered non-exempt employees was $6.55 per hour, as of 24 July 2008.

9 For a good recent discussion of the impact of migration on wages, see J. Hardy, 'Migration, Migrant Workers and Capitalism', *International Socialism*, Spring 2009.

10 For further discussion of countervailing forces, see D. Harvey, *Limits to Capital*, Verso, 2006, pp. 178, 179. See also Choonara, *Unravelling Capitalism*, pp. 79–83.

11 Larry Elliott and Dan Atkinson warned consistently of the pitfalls in globalisation. See L. Elliot & D. Atkinson, *Fantasy Island*, Constable, 2007, pp. 36–7, 84, 94, 204, 231. See also Larry Elliott, 'Is free trade the best way to beat recession?', *Guardian*, 4 February 2009.

12 Martin Wolf, chief economics commentator of the *Financial Times*, was one who certainly worried about the rise of extreme trade imbalances. See 'A dangerous hunger for American assets', *Financial Times*, 7 December 2003. He continued to warn about these imbalances six years later. See 'Why G20 leaders will fail to deal with the big challenge', *Financial Times*, 31 March 2009. However, as argued in *The Credit Crunch*, focusing on the current account imbalances as a response to excess savings missed the point about globalisation and the contribution of increased trade to the rise of these deficits. Failure to see this underlying problem led many commentators to underestimate the scale of the looming financial crisis when in it broke in 2007. See G. Turner, *The Credit Crunch*, Pluto Press, 2008, Chapter 4.

13 Source: Bureau of Economic Analysis (BEA). US Corporate Profits with Inventory Valuation Adjustment (IVA) and Capital Consumption Adjustment (CCADJ)/GDP rose to a post-war peak of 13.3 per cent in Q4 1950. It reached a cyclical high of 12.9 per cent in Q3 2006. Domestic Non-financial Profits with IVA and CCADJ/GDP reached a high of 7.5 per cent in Q3 2006, compared with a peak of 11.8 per cent in Q4 1950.

14 Marx, *Capital*, Volume 3, p. 398. 'The identity of surplus value and surplus labour imposes a quantitative limit upon the accumulation of capital. That consists of the working day... But if one conceives of surplus-value in the meaningless form of interest, the limit is merely quantitative and defies all imagination.'

15 Source: National Bureau of Statistics, China. Gross Fixed Capital Formation as a percentage of Gross Domestic Product was 42.0 per cent in 2008.

16 Source: Thomson Reuters Datastream. On 10 July 2005, the renminbi (R) was allowed by the People's Bank of China to start appreciating against the US dollar ($). It rose steadily from R/$8.2765 to a high of R/$6.8009 on 23 September 2008. By 26 June 2009, the renminbi had fallen against the US dollar, to R/$6.8328.

17 Source: Ministry of Finance, Japan. Exports of Goods, Customs Basis, fell 47.8 per cent between January 2008 and February 2009.

18 Source: Ministry of Economy, Trade and Industry, Industrial Production, Manufacturing.

19 See *Historical Statistics of the United States, Colonial Times to 1970, Part 2*, US Department of Commerce, Bureau of the Census, p. 667.

20 See *Historical Statistics of the United States, Colonial Times to 1970, Part 1*, US Department of Commerce, Bureau of the Census, p. 224.

21 Source: Cabinet Office (Japan), GDP, Yen Billion (2000 prices).

22 Source: Ministry of Economic Affairs, Taiwan. Industrial Production fell 43.3 per cent y/y in January 2009. Source: Bank of Thailand. Manufacturing Production dropped 21.2 per cent y/y in January 2009. Source: National Statistics Office, South Korea. Industrial Production fell 25.5 per cent y/y in January 2009. Source: Department of Statistics, Singapore. Industrial Production excluding rubber processing dropped 29.8 per cent y/y in January 2009. Source: Department of Statistics, Malaysia. Industrial Production shrank 17.9 per cent y/y in January 2009.

23 Source: Statistisches Bundesamt.

24 Source: Deutsche Bundesbank.

25 Source: Eurostat. The peak for Finland was March 2006.

26 Source: Eurostat.

27 Source: Federal Reserve, Office for National Statistics and Eurostat. Euroland (EA 16) Industrial Production fell 20.7 per cent y/y in March 2009, compared with a drop of 12.7 per cent y/y in the US and 12.3 per cent y/y in the UK.

28 Source: Cabinet Office (Japan), Operating Ratio, Manufacturing.

29 Source: Federal Reserve.

30   Source: Confederation of British Industry (CBI) Enquiry: Percentage Working Below Capacity.
31   Source: Ministry of Finance. Incorporated Business, Current Profits – All Industries, fell 69.0 per cent y/y in Q1 2009.
32   Source: Ministry of Finance. Incorporated Business, Current Profits – Manufacturing, fell 141.7 per cent y/y in Q1 2009, to *minus* ¥2.246 trillion.
33   Source: Corporate Net Cash Flow fell 24.5 per cent q/q in Q4 2008, before rising 10.5 per cent q/q in Q1 2009.
34   Source: Federal Reserve. Industrial Utilisation – Manufacturing, reached a high of 79.6 per cent in April and August 2006. That compares with an average of 81.0 per cent between January 1950 and May 2009.
35   Source: Deutsche Bundesbank. Manufacturing Orders had fallen 48.3 per cent by April 2009, compared with the June 2007 peak. In the three months to April 2009, they were down 44.4 per cent y/y.
36   Source: Cabinet Office (Japan). Machinery Orders, Foreign Demand, dropped 74.4 per cent y/y in February 2009.
37   Harvey, *Limits to Capital*, pp. 296–305.
38   C. Harman, *Zombie Capitalism, Global Crisis and the Relevance of Marx*, Bookmarks Publications, 2009, pp. 166–70. See also Choonara, *Unravelling Capitalism*, pp. 134–6.
39   Source: BEA, %, US Corporate Profits with Inventory Valuation Adjustment and Capital Consumption Adjustment/Nominal GDP.
40   Source: BEA, %, US Corporate Profits with Inventory Valuation Adjustment and Capital Consumption Adjustment/Non-Residential Private Fixed Investment.
41   For more, see Harvey, *Limits to Capital*, pp. 180, 181.
42   Source: BEA, %, US Corporate Profits with Inventory Valuation Adjustment and Capital Consumption Adjustment, Rest of the World/Domestic Industries. This ratio fell to 40.6 per cent in Q1 2009.
43   Source: BEA, %, US Corporate Profits with Inventory Valuation Adjustment and Capital Consumption Adjustment, Domestic Non-Financial/Domestic Industries. This ratio rebounded from 14.1 per cent in Q4 2008 to 25.3 per cent in Q1 2009.
44   Source: BEA, %, US Corporate Profits with Inventory Valuation Adjustment and Capital Consumption Adjustment, Domestic Non-Financial/Non-Residential Private Fixed Investment. This ratio peaked at 120.6 per cent in Q4 1950 and then reached a cyclical high of 69.6 per cent in Q3 2006 following the housing boom. It fell to 49.6 per cent in Q4 2008 before rebounding to 52.3 per cent in Q1 2009.

45   Source: BEA, %, US Real Non-Residential Private Fixed Investment/
     Real GDP. This ratio fell to 10.5 per cent in Q1 2009.

Chapter 6

1   G. Tily, *Keynes's General Theory, The Rate of Interest and 'Keynesian'
    Economics*, Palgrave Macmillan, 2007, p. 32.
2   The Marxist critique of Keynes, has always been, at its root, a critique
    of his methodology, in particular his 'marginalist' framework. See
    C. Harman, 'The Crisis of Bourgeois Economics', *International
    Socialism*, June 1996.
3   Ibid. The shift away from Keynes's prescription is recognised by
    Chris Harman in 'The Crisis of Bourgeois Economics'. And there
    is, of course, an open question of what would have happened if a
    true Keynes prescription had been applied in the early 1970s. Even
    if such policies had headed off stagflation, the emerging structural
    crisis – that is, the secular decline in the profit rate – would have
    manifested itself in other ways.
4   Ibid. Some Marxist economists argue that Keynes's policies did not
    go far enough during the late 1930s, because his solutions were
    'pragmatically' tailored to what he believed politicians would
    accept.
5   Tily, *Keynes's General Theory, The Rate of Interest and 'Keynesian'
    Economics*, p. 301.
6   Ibid., p. 89. 'If the prevailing long-term tap rate becomes chronically
    too low, in the sense that it encourages new capital formation on a
    scale tending to inflation, the rate should, in general be raised.'
7   Ibid., p. 314. 'For Keynes was above all concerned with international
    and domestic monetary reform.'
8   Ibid., p. 318.
9   Ibid., p. 314. 'The vast majority of Keynes' contributions to economic
    theory were concerned with monetary economics.'
10 D. Harvey, *Limits to Capital*, Verso, 2006, p. 295.
11 See '"Global awakening" is fuelling gains in asset markets', *Financial
    Times*, 31 May 2007, Marc Chandler, Brown Brothers Harriman
    and Jim Glassman, JP Morgan and Chase.
12 M. Friedman & A.J. Schwartz, *A Monetary History of the United
    States, 1867–1960*, Princeton University Press, 1963, p. 412.
13 Ibid., p. 412.
14 Ibid., p. 412.
15 Ibid., pp. 412–13.
16 Ibid., p. 413.
17 Ibid., p. 418.

Chapter 7

1   See Lawrence Summers, 'Why America must have a fiscal stimulus', *Financial Times*, 6 January 2008. Mr Summers was appointed Director of the National Economic Council in January 2009.

2   Source: Department of Commerce. Disposable Personal Income rose 5.7 per cent m/m in May 2008. Real Personal Consumption rose 2.5 per cent m/m in May 2008. But disposable incomes fell thereafter, dragging consumer spending down in each of the next five months. By November 2008, Real Personal Consumption was falling at a 3m/3m annualised rate of 4.6 per cent.

3   Source: Thomson Reuters Datastream and Mortgage Bankers Association. The US Treasury Benchmark Bond 10-Year Yield rose from 3.31 per cent on 17 March 2008 to a high of 4.26 per cent on 13 June 2008. The Conventional Mortgage Contract Rate, 30-Year, climbed from a low of 5.49 per cent in the third week of January 2008 to 6.59 per cent in the fourth week of July 2008.

4   See 'How late is too late?', Paul Krugman, *New York Times*, 27 January 2009. See also interview with Paul Krugman, BBC World News America, 12 February 2009, 'The stimulus plan is a lot better than nothing, but it's not as big as it ought to be, and not as well-focused as it ought to be.' http://news.bbc.co.uk/1/hi/programmes/world_news_america/7885019.stm, accessed 7 July 2009. See also 'Paul Krugman's fear for lost decade', *Observer*, 14 June 2009. Mr Krugman played down the significance of the rise in bond yields over the spring and summer of 2009, claiming that this merely reflected higher inflation expectations. His failure to recognise the significance of this bond market sell-off exposes a critical lack of understanding in the way Keynes's policies were meant to work.

5   A. Posen, *Restoring Japan's Economic Growth*, Institute for International Economics, September 1998, pp. 29–51.

6   Source: Ministry of Internal Affairs & Communication, Japan. The Consumer Price Index excluding Food and Energy (Core) fell 0.5 per cent y/y in May 2009, compared with 0.0 per cent y/y in December 2008. That is still above the low of 1.1 per cent y/y set in March 2001. But the Tokyo Consumer Price Index excluding Fresh Food dropped more quickly in June 2009, by 1.3 per cent y/y, compared with a fall of 0.7 per cent y/y in May, suggesting that the deflation rate in Japan was still intensifying.

7   Source: Japan Real Estate Institute with Thomson Reuters Datastream calculations. A further fall of 4.2 per cent from the level reached in Q1 2009 would take the Nationwide Land Price Index down to its lowest level since Q3 1973.

8   G. Turner, *Solutions to a Liquidity Trap*, GFC Economics, 2003, pp. 169–74 and G. Turner, *The Credit Crunch*, Pluto Press, 2008, pp. 159–67.

9   Source: Organisation for Economic Co-operation and Development (OECD), General Government Financial Balance/Nominal GDP. The worst year for Japan's budget deficit was 1998, when it reached 11.2 per cent of GDP. That compares with an expected shortfall of 12.4 per cent of GDP in the UK for Fiscal Year 2009 and an expected deficit of 12.8 per cent of GDP in the US, for Fiscal Year 2009.

10   Source: Thomson Reuters Datastream. The differential between 10-Year Government Bond Yields (Japanese Government Bonds, JGBs) and the Discount Rate in Japan was 2.93 per cent in August 1994. By contrast, the differential between the 10-Year Government Bond Yield (Gilts) and the Base Rate in the UK rose to 3.80 per cent in May 2009. The differential between the 10-Year Government Bond Yields in the US and the Federal Reserve Funds Target rose to 3.61 per cent in June 2009.

11   Source: Federal Reserve, Flow of Funds (FoF), Table L.107, Rest of the World. At the end of Q4 2008, overseas investors held $3,187.4 billion of US Treasury Securities. Official investors held $2,125.1 billion, while private investors held $1,062.2 billion.

12   G. Tily, *Keynes's General Theory, the Rate of Interest and 'Keynesian' Economics*, Palgrave Macmillan, 2007, pp. 76–7, 202–3, 223.

13   See 'Credit card losses hit record 10.4%', *Financial Times*, 30 June 2009.

14   Source: Federal Reserve, Federal Financial Institutions Examination Council. A report for Q1 2009 showed that Delinquency Rates, Total Loans & Leases, climbed from 4.64 per cent (in Q4 2008) to 5.60 per cent, a rise of 0.96 per cent. That was a record increase. By contrast, Charge-Off Rates for Total Loans & Leases rose from 1.90 per cent in Q4 2008 to 2.04 per cent in Q1 2009, a rise of just 0.14 per cent. This was the smallest increase since Q4 2007.

15   See 'Libor hits record low as credit fears ease', *Financial Times*, 5 May 2009.

16   Source: Thomson Reuters Datastream. The 3-Month Inter-bank Offered Rate for US Dollars fell to 0.59 per cent on 30 June 2009. For Sterling, it dropped to 1.19 per cent. For Euros, it fell to 1.09 per cent.

17   See 'Brown wades into Rock row', Channel 4 News, 17 October 2008. www.channel4.com/news/articles/business_money/brown+wades+into+rock+row/2557477, accessed 7 July 2009.

18   See 'Northern Rock losses grow by more than £500m', *Daily Telegraph*, 1 July 2009.

19 See 'Federal National Mortgage Association' Quarterly Report, Q1
    2009, p. 50. Net interest income was $1.69 billion in Q1 2008 and
    rose to $3.25 billion in Q1 2009. Credit-related expenses were $3.24
    billion in Q1 2008, and climbed to $20.88 billion in Q1 2009. Net
    loss was $2.19 billion in Q1 2008 and rose to $23.19 billion in
    Q1 2009.

20 Fannie Mae introduced two moratoria, one from 26 November
    2008 to 31 January 2009 and a second from 17 February 2009 to
    6 March 2009.

21 The dispersion of bonds through securitisation has been a major
    handicap in securing lower payments on mortgages. Ultimately,
    legislation will be required to make lower payments possible. The
    potential, negative short run impact on bond prices should be
    outweighed by the prospect of some stabilisation in house prices,
    which would eventually raise the value of these bonds.

22 See Willem Buiter, 'Quantitative easing, credit easing and enhanced
    credit support aren't working; here's why', *Financial Times*, 3 July
    2009. Mr Buiter makes a number of basic errors in his 'analysis'
    of quantitative easing, and then concludes that banks need greater
    injections of capital.

23 Turner, *Solutions to a Liquidity Trap*, pp. 69–71, 84.

24 See C. Harman, 'The Slump of the 1930s and the Crisis Today',
    International Socialism, Winter 2009, pp. 38–45. Chris Harman
    correctly argues that there were deeper structural causes behind
    Japan's bear market, including a sharp drop in profit rates between
    the 1960s and 1970s.

25 Turner, *Solutions to a Liquidity Trap*, pp. 153–7.

26 See Note 14 for more.

Chapter 8

1 J.M. Keynes, *The General Theory of Employment, Interest and
   Money*, Macmillan Cambridge University Press, 1936, pp. 5–18,
   21–2, 259, 284.

2 Source: *Historical Statistics of the United States, Colonial Times to
   1970*, US Department of Commerce, Bureau of the Census, Part 1, p.
   224 and Part 2, p. 1105. The peak US deficit of 28.1 per cent of GDP
   was in 1943. Source: C.H. Feinstein, *National Income, Expenditure
   & Output of the UK 1855–1965*, Cambridge University Press, 1972,
   T10, T35. The peak UK deficit was 26.1 per cent of GDP in 1941.

3 Source: *Historical Statistics of the United States, Colonial Times to
   1970*, Part 1, p. 224 and Part 2, p. 1105.

4   See 'Oral Evidence Taken Before The Treasury Committee', House of Commons, 10 February 2009. www.publications.parliament.uk/pa/cm200809/cmselect/cmtreasy/uc144_vii/uc14402.htm, accessed 9 July 2009.

5   See 'Tesco's pledge: We will double in size', *London Evening Standard*, 21 April 2009.

6   See R. Brenner & M. Probsting, *The Credit Crunch: A Marxist Analysis*, Fifth International, 2008, p. 96. See also J. Choonara, *Unravelling Capitalism*, Bookmarks Publications, May 2009, pp. 90–4.

7   Source: Thomson Reuters Datastream. The Dow Jones Industrials Price Index closed at 8447.0 on 30 June 2009. It climbed above this level on 29 October 1998. The FTSE 100 Price Index closed at 4249.2 on 30 June 2009. It climbed above this level on 7 April 1997.

8   Source: Federal Reserve, Industrial Production, Aircraft & Parts and Manufacturing.

9   See 'Health risks of shipping pollution have been "underestimated"', *Guardian*, 9 April 2009.

INDEX